GW00480512

Cats Can Fly

Brian Heath

purchaser.

A CIP catalogue record for this title is available from the British Library.

Introduction

This is the story of a jack of all trades, a headbanger, someone who has tilted at more windmills than Don Quixote ever saw, but whose philosophy has always been to turn adversities into, in some way, an opportunity to sidestep and find different solutions. Not always possible in many cases to do this but, if so, to throw oneself in a different way to keep the monkey off one's back. Over the past few years, friends and relatives have suggested that I write down some of this stuff when I have time, especially my wonderful partner of some 12 years. When she arrived home after shopping, in February this year, with a foolscap (appropriate name!) book and half a dozen Biro pens I had no further excuse and so a 98-year-old guy has written his first book, starting before the Covid-19 lockdown and finishing it in six months. I hope it will not bore you if you have been foolish enough to obtain it. Some consolation, all money made (if any) will go to Julia's House Children's Hospice. A magnificent charity that I admire tremendously.

Brian

2020

Contents

Early Days

I cannot remember not being fascinated by rhythm and, although I don't remember this, I was told that as soon as I was old enough to sit at the table and use a spoon and fork if there was music playing on the radio I would be rattling the spoon and fork on the table. As parents do, I was offered a bribe, that if I could behave at the table and mind my manners they would buy me a toy drum for my birthday. I do remember that drum, a tin one with small drumsticks and I was over the moon, what joy! I don't remember the awful racket I must have made to begin with, but I later recall trying to beat out the rhythm of simple nursery rhymes. I was more interested in the beat than the lyrics as they do have a lovely lilt to them and after all, a mouse running up and down a clock isn't going to make the ten o'clock news, but the rhythm is great. Eventually, I practised so that I could beat out a nursery rhyme and ask Alan, my older brother, or my mother to identify the tune. I never asked my dad because he was a proper musician and I thought it would be beneath his dignity.

I then began to realise that if I let the sticks bounce I

Hainsworth Heath my Dad

could get a rough approximation of a drum roll. I practised this and as I got a little older, I could get a reasonable sound. At this stage, my parents got me a basic drum instruction book, but I never had lessons as we lived in a small village in the Yorkshire Wolds and although my dad had a semi-pro dance/jazz band the musicians were spread over what, at that time, was considered a large area and only got together rarely for rehearsals, which happily I was allowed to sit and listen to. This would be in the late 1920s when I was seven or eight years old. My dad was born in 1885 and started playing for dances on violin and piano in 1900. He formed a band in the late 1920s and it varied from a trio to an eight-piece band according to the venue and when it was the full eight-

10

piece band, four of the band members were from the Heath family. At around this time, Ted Heath[1] was playing trombone with Jack Hylton and later with Ambrose, who knows we may have been related!

One evening the drummer in the band asked if I would like a kiddies little drum set which he had no more use for, the set, a small drum with a pedal, a snare drum, a little tom-tom and a small brass cymbal. I was delighted with it and began to practice to about half a dozen 78 rpm records, which my parents let me play on our old gramophone. I remember its huge green metal horn and I had to promise to be very careful when using it. One of the records was a trick record with three tracks and one of the tracks was a rather up-tempo version of Farewell Blues and this was what inspired me to really work on my technique and to appreciate jazz music. With these old gramophones, it was possible to slow the speed of

---

[1] Ted Heath went on to form what is widely considered Britain's greatest post-war big band, recording more than 100 albums, which sold over 20 million copies. In the 1930s Ted played with Jack Hylton who was referred as the 'British King of Jazz' and Ambrose, who was the leader of a highly acclaimed British dance band, 'Bert Ambrose and His Orchestra'.

rotation down and by doing this, I could follow the drum breaks and then speed it up as I got better. The only problem with this is that it affects the pitch more than the tempo, so that made Louis Armstrong sound like he's playing the tuba! When I was 11 years old in 1933, the drummer in the band got a job in Leeds and the hours were not such that he could play nights, so my dad asked me if I would like to try playing in the band. Of course I would and it was at that stage I got my first paid gig, but more of this later.

Another early memory is a love of anything on wheels or wings or both for that matter. I'm told that the first thing I tried to draw was two crude circles with a line through them saying "KA – KA" excitedly, which turned out to be quite prophetic. Something I don't remember is that as a toddler I was stung by a bee, which had got caught in my hair. I must have tried to brush it off and hurt it so it stung me on my head and probably buzzed quite loudly.

What occurred later is my earliest memory and I hesitate to describe it, but it did happen, so here goes. I started having nightmares and would wake up screaming every night. I remember clearly I dreamt that a huge bee about eighteen inches long was flying down a corridor towards my bedroom. I slammed the door but too late, the bee was trapped halfway in and was buzzing loudly and gradually forcing itself through the doorway, try as I might to stop it. In those days, there was a lot of those tiny flies that we used to call wine flies and they used to hover near one's ear, probably thinking it would be a good place to kip down for the night. They made a high-pitched buzzing noise, which may have caused my dream. My parents ran the local village shop and Post Office and had to rise at 5:30 am to start the day. They had no staff, so my mother needed help to do the housework etc. They employed a young teenage girl who lived in and slept in a single bedroom between my parents' and mine. This young lady offered to help by coming into my bed to comfort me when I had these nightmares.

For years after I believed what happened next was a recurring dream night after night which was much better than the bee thing so I didn't worry about it. This 'dream' was that someone was placing my hand on to a totally inappropriate place and if my hand moved away it was gently but firmly replaced. I could not understand it but it was better than the bee nightmare. I don't remember how long this 'dream' lasted, but eventually, this girl was replaced so I guess my parents may have found out and that was that. The girl, a year or two later, became an unmarried mother but I can assure you that I was not involved!

Both my parents were from farming stock and were the eldest of large families and as seemed to be the case in those days they were both over forty when they married. My mum was the eldest of twelve and was expected to help with the daily chores and to look after her younger siblings, which she did with loving care and Dad was the eldest of nine and would have probably inherited my Grandad's rented farm, but he had a very serious bout of pneumonia, which left him with a weak heart, so although he started to work on the farm he wasn't fit enough. However, he had been very good at school and he went to a school in Scarborough to finish his education and this enabled him to take over a village shop and Post Office after he and Mum were married.

Buying the shop meant taking out a bank loan and I remember worried looks and difficult times when the monthly interest became due. This was in the late 1920s and early 1930s when there were periods of deflation, which meant that goods were sold at less than the wholesale price. They tried all kinds of things to help and even though there was no mains electricity in the village, they sold fish and chips in winter. I remember a huge chip pan on the kitchen range, which needed careful handling and Mum cooking the fish using a paraffin

The Post Office, Foxholes

stove in the back kitchen. They also did ice cream in the summer. They bought ice from a travelling fishmonger so it was only one day a week. The village wasn't very large and about 95% of the occupants were farmworkers on low wages, so ice cream was a luxury not everyone could afford. My mum tried stocking drapery and once a week, when a local village bus ran, she would call at nearby villages with two cases of draperies. My dad, having had piano and violin lessons at Scarborough school was able to help finances by running the semi-pro band playing mainly for dances. In 1900 at the age of 15, he started playing for dances where the ladies were given a small booklet complete with a little silver capped pencil and the ladies would book their dances with various partners and it was not good form to dance with the same partner all evening. They danced the Schottische Minuet and the rather daring Viennese Waltz. All very sedate, so it must have been rather daunting for a 15-year-old playing for the first time. In the late 1920s, he formed the 'Heath Orchestra' his first eight-piece band. I believe that at that time Ted Heath was busking on the London

Streets and one of my ancestors was a Sir Thomas Heath[2], a former member of the Cabinet so I understand.

Initially the eight-piece band had four members of the Heath family in it and in 1933 one of them left but I joined the band so I kept up the percentage. I continued to play drums with the band and I will never forget my first gig. It was a Post Office dinner and dance and it went on from 10 pm to 2 am! A very tired little 11-year-old, but so excited and I got a lovely crisp 10 shilling note! I also remember decorating my drum kit with red, white and blue ribbons for a special dance to celebrate the Silver Jubilee of King George V in 1935.

As time went on my dad started getting problems with arthritis and couldn't do the fingering so well. He was a perfectionist so he decided to ease off, and so, rather than see the band fail I took it over at the age of 16. During

---

[2] Sir Thomas Little Heath KCB KCVO FRS FBA 1861-1940 was a civil servant, mathematician, classical scholar, historian of ancient Greek mathematics, translator and mountaineer. He was Brian's second cousin twice removed. There is a grand painting of Sir Thomas and Ada, Lady Heath in the National Portrait Gallery. Their house "Merry Hall" was later owned and popularised by the writer Beverley Nichols in a book of the same name.

the next two years, we became more of a jazz band, but we were OK because a lot of the younger generation had seen 'Jitterbugging' on film from the USA. In 1939 an army searchlight unit arrived nearby and two lads from it came to a gig we were doing. One of them asked if he could go on the piano in the interval, we said OK and he, with his pal on guitar were really great, Fats Waller style. I thought I'd like him and I asked him if he could swap shifts with his mates, so I gave him some dates. One of the problems where we lived was to find good musicians so when I heard him I didn't hesitate. We did the next three gigs as a trio or quartet and it went down really well. Unfortunately, I went into the RAF and on my first leave, I found that the three lads had moved on and I lost touch with them.

For some reason, jazz musicians were and maybe still are, known as 'cats' and dancers were 'hep cats'. Now cats are reputed to have nine lives and I can say with good reason that I have used up eight of mine, which I will now describe in detail.

Life Number 1 - Water

When I was born my dad was working on Grandad Heath's tenanted farm with a fairly large farmhouse. My mother decided when I was a baby, that as it was a lovely day she would put me in the pram outside the front door, on what was believed to be a piece of level ground. Now prams in those days were deep-bodied with small wheels, solid rubber thin tyres and no brakes. She chocked the wheels with two large stones and left me to enjoy the lovely day. I guess I must have bounced around a bit although I was strapped in. Maybe I was thinking - I've got wheels at last! I must have rocked the pram enough to dislodge the stones and the ground was not level as was thought. The pram slowly rolled off the level bit and gathered speed, as the ground fell away, it also turned as it went until it was heading straight for the farmyard pond! As luck would have it my Uncle Wilf, who also worked on the farm happened to come round the corner of a barn with a 16 stone bag of corn on his back, just in time to spot the pram handles disappear under the water! Two seconds later and there would have been no trace. He dropped the sack and raced to the pond and could see the course the pram had taken by a disturbance of the green slime on the surface of the pond. He managed to find the handles and pull me out, unstrapped me and put me face down over his knee, giving my back a gentle thump causing me to return the pond to its previous level and possibly discharging a few tadpoles and a little frogspawn as well. A few years later I used to be fascinated watching the horses drinking huge quantities of the water after a hard day's work in the fields, but they would filter the water between their teeth. Whereas I didn't have any teeth on my visit to the pond!

Life Number 2 - More Water

After my parents moved to the village shop, on Sundays my brother Alan and I used to go on lovely walks down country lanes with Mum and Dad. One time we saw a mother partridge trying to lead us after her by

pretending to have a broken wing and when she decided that her ploy had succeeded she just flew off back to her chicks. We also saw a lapwing parent doing the same thing, its chick was absolutely still so we could only see it by not taking our

Alan and myself 1928

eyes off it, the camouflage was perfect.

Life went happily by although Alan, who was two years older than I, started to be troubled by asthma and impetigo. He wasn't able to take part in the usual sports which were mainly cricket and football. However, he became very studious and while I would get the 'Champion' comic he got 'Modern Boy' which was a very good introduction to science (Dandy and Beano were not invented then). We both went to the village school which was very basic. It consisted of two rooms, the infants and the big room, as it was called. There were only two teachers: the infants had a young girl not qualified and the other teacher who was qualified but had a roomful of kids to teach aged 9½ to the school leaving age of 14 on all subjects including religion as it was a C of E school. This was of course an impossible task and from the age of 12 to 14 it was a case of working if you felt like it, but most kids did not. It was 95% farming country and the lads couldn't wait to go on one of the farms and the girls as housemaids or milkmaids.

During the school holidays we could go to a relative, such as an uncle or aunt and play with our cousins, or they would come to us. None of us could afford holidays otherwise. It didn't matter as we lived fairly near to the sea and Uncle Fred was stationmaster at Goathland which was then part of the LNER line to Whitby. Part of his duties was to inspect a long stretch of line on foot and we always enjoyed accompanying him as it was such lovely scenery with lots of wildlife. We kids had a rather naughty episode once when we put a halfpenny on the line and after the engine and carriages went over it the halfpenny was now thin and almost a penny size (nowadays kids put sleepers on the line).

Alan, Freda, Me and Dot at Harwood Dale around 1930

On one of my holidays, when I was about eight or nine years old, I was staying with my Auntie Dot's family in Scalby, a village just north of Scarborough and just a short walk to a fairly quiet little bay. My two cousins who were a little older than I took me down to a small sandy beach. The eldest one (also called Dot) was considered old enough to look after us whilst my Uncle and Auntie ran their stall in Scarborough market.

It was a lovely day and we played most of the afternoon, perfect conditions for building castles in the sand. There was also a large diameter pipe running almost parallel to the waterline. This was taking raw sewage from Scarborough to a few miles up the coast so that the good beaches in the town were not polluted. This pipe, about 4½ ft in diameter formed a barrier to the sea, which was almost up to the top of the pipe on the seaward side, but only about knee-deep on the landward side. As kids do, mostly lads, in this case, it was a dare to run along the top of the round pipe as it emerged from the rocks on one side to where it was again buried in the land after about 50 yards or so. The pipe was a bit slippery with green algae, especially on the seaward side. I was very apprehensive about doing it, but didn't want to be called a cowardy custard! So with my heart in my mouth, I started my run. Unfortunately, a bigger lad appeared coming in the opposite direction. We collided and both fell off. He was on the landward side and me on the deeper seaward side. I couldn't swim and could only just keep my nose above water if I stood on my toes and then not when a wave came. I struggled to try and climb the pipe but to no avail. After what seemed like a lifetime I was absolutely exhausted and had swallowed a fair bit of seawater. My fingernails were torn and finger ends were raw, but the pipe was too slippery. I felt that awful certainty that I would just have to let go and without any energy left I had no option. Dot had been concentrating on building a huge sandcastle, but for a moment she looked for me to show me her handiwork. She couldn't see me but saw a hand flailing above the top of the pipe. Dot and her sister, Freda, ran to the pipe and just managed to clutch my hand before I drifted away. The two of them managed to pull me up so that I was draped over the top of the pipe and then managed to get me over the top. They carried me up the beach where, once again I was able to return a body of water, in this case, North Sea, back to its normal level. I was dressed in shirt and shorts which were of course soaked. They dragged me back to their house and dried me off, put me to bed where I stayed for two weeks, developed a temperature and felt as weak as a kitten.

Now I don't remember the farmyard pond episode, but this one I remember as if it was yesterday. This gave me a lifelong dread of getting my head below water and, on subsequent visits to the seaside, I never went deeper than waist-high, even then feeling uncomfortable when the waves receded giving that slight pull. Little did I know what life had in store for me.

Wings and Wheels

As we got little or no homework from school I was able to put more time into practising my drumming and also reading everything I could about cars, motorbikes and aeroplanes. One of my heroes was Freddie Dixon, a garage mechanic who competed in a hill climb at Staxton Hill near our home. As a very young kid, I was taken to watch him and apparently burst into tears at the noise, my parents pulled my leg but later I insisted that I was cheering! Freddie was a real character, but also very clever at tuning the inlet and exhaust lengths to get the maximum airflow through the cylinders. Later, when he raced cars with a multi-cylinder car engine he was one of the first to have an Amal motorcycle carburettor to each cylinder. He went to great lengths to keep this to himself, locking the bonnet to prevent anyone seeing what he had done. Later after a successful career, he was charged with, I think, drink driving and had a spell in jail. During this time a national newspaper reported that he was tuning police cars, but later he said this was not true, if he had been doing that he would have to make sure that police cars didn't catch anyone! In his early days, he was riding a motorbike and sidecar with three mates on board en route to a nearby pub. He started a bet that the last one into the pub bought the beer. The other lads thought they were onto a good thing as Freddie was riding the bike, but as they approached the pub Freddie leapt off the bike before it had stopped, leaving them to scramble over to shut the throttle down – of course he won the bet!

When I was about nine and Alan eleven, my parents took us to see Alan Cobham's Flying Circus as it was popularly known, which was set up in a large fairly flat field at Grindale just outside Bridlington. We were thrilled to see a wonderful exhibition of flying by some very gifted pilots, a few of them became very well known later. We were given the option of a short flight but it was quite expensive, five shillings each and we thought it was too much, that we were lucky to be taken to the show, where there was proper wing walking with no harness. One plane picking up a handkerchief off a small peg on the ground with a spike on his wingtip - wonderful! There was also a static showpiece, the Golden Arrow car, the world's land speed record holder at the time. It was the most beautiful thing I had ever seen. There was a notice, please do not touch as it was very polished, but after a quick look round, I did touch one of its front tyres, something I was able to repeat at Beaulieu Motor Museum about 85 years later, where the car was on display.

This wonderful event gave Alan and I a lifelong interest in flying. We went to another event, a nearby air race around three village church spires. The star of this meeting was Alex Henshaw who became world-famous, breaking numerous long-distance flying records, notably in a Percival Mew Gull, a lovely little plane. He went on to be a test pilot, mainly Spitfires, during WW2. Alex was a young, handsome guy and he became our hero, he flew a little Comper Swift single-seat plane. Alan made his first scale model of the Comper Swift, the first of a series of very fine scale models. His final one, a wonderfully detailed model of the Halifax bomber he flew in as flight engineer. Alan completed a full tour of operations and these were marked on the fuselage of the model, which at 1:72 scale were tiny. It had a revolving rear turret with the four machine guns able to be moved up and down together, even though at that scale the guns were about a quarter the thickness of a pin. In those days there were no model kits and the fuselage was made from lard boxes. The gun turrets and the cockpit canopy were made from offcuts of Perspex so they were from original material.

In the late 1930s, Alan and I did a lot of cycling on

Bank Holidays and once a year a two-week tour; the first one touring Mid and North Wales, using some rather hairy mountain passes. On the descent of one of these, my handlebars became detached from the stem! Luckily I had cable brakes and was able to pull up, but as I had toe-clips I just had to roll off onto a grass verge.

One even more worrying thing, we left the bikes at the youth hostel and ascended Mt Snowdon by foot. However, Alan scorned using the established paths to find our own, more direct route to the top. When we started to descend, again making our own way, suddenly we were engulfed in thick cloud. We followed a tiny stream but suddenly it disappeared into a rocky part and we were unable to follow it. I was really scared and by this time we were soaked to the skin. Somehow we got back to the hostel much to my relief.

A few days later we were descending a steep winding hill in the Lake District. Alan was riding an upright bike whereas I was on one with dropped handlebars, this would give me a lower centre of gravity and he was ahead of me when we encountered a sharp left-hand hairpin bend. Alan didn't make it and shot off the road, I just made it and saw Alan dodging boulders over bumpy ground! Then came a right-hand hairpin bend and as I straightened up there was Alan rejoining the road, still ahead of me!

The next summer we planned to go down to London. Alan wanted to visit the Science Museum and I the Herne Hill cycle track to see world-class sprinters doing their stuff. En route we planned to visit Donnington Park to see the British Grand Prix motor race, where the all-conquering Mercedes and Auto Unions were representing Germany. But owing to the critical political climate the event was postponed and instead, we saw a smaller race for what would now be considered Formula 2. Nevertheless, I enjoyed seeing my first motor race and saw the English ERAs (English Racing Automobiles Ltd) racing against French Bugattis and Italian Alfa Romeos. In London, I think I enjoyed the Science Museum more than Alan did the cycle racing, but we were both happy to do things together.

On the way back North we planned to use as many coastal roads or tracks as possible and were staying at youth hostels each evening. At one of these hostels, a smallish one where the warden lived nearby, we were the only two British lads there. The other dozen or so were all well-built, blond-haired German lads, probably Hitler Youth. We didn't chat to them or them to us, the atmosphere was cool but calm. After what happened later I wondered if they were not exactly spies, but on a fact-finding mission to report on the British Chain Home stations, a series of huge masts about 60-70 miles apart up the East coast. But more of that later.

After war was declared, Alan volunteered to train as a pilot but did not meet the education requirement. He was very brainy and had qualified as an architect in Scarborough, one of their star pupils, but he had not been to grammar school. This was the minimum requirement at the outset of WW2 for aircrew training as pilot or navigator. Although he had been to the small village school he had taught himself calculus before he left school at 14 years old and could have passed any exams. He initially trained as a fitter on ground staff and spent the next 15 months working as a fitter.

By the time I was old enough to volunteer because the RAF had lost so many brave pilots in the Battle of Britain and Bomber Command, they had to lower the level of qualification and if you could pass a fairly simple written exam you were accepted for training. However, in my case, there were about six months from passing the exam and being called up. It was arranged for me to make weekly visits to be seen by the headmaster of Bridlington

Grammar School who gave me a week's work to help me. I learned more from him about Maths and Physics than I had learned in the last two years at the village school.

In Alan's case, after his 15 months as a fitter, he applied again for flying training, but they would only take him on as Flight Engineer because of his experience as a fitter. He trained and then joined a Halifax four-engined bomber squadron. They did a full 30 plus sorties. It was a 100% successful tour and the pilot got a DFC (Distinguished Flying Cross) as they had found and bombed every target successfully.

By this time I had started my training and it began by attending ACRC (Air Crew Receiving Centre) at Lord's cricket ground. As I approached the gates there was an old man seated on a bench saying over and over again "You'll be sorry." There were times later when I wondered if he had a point. There were huge queues but I eventually got into the main building where we were shown into the famous Long Room where three medical officers were conducting a process known as FFI (Free From Infection) which involved dropping pants while the MOs (Medical Officers) did a quick inspection of our nether regions and all under the stern features of the great

W.G. Grace frowning down from his huge portrait!

The next three weeks were doing foot drill, but also we discovered that our flight was classed as requiring eye training which was mainly standing on a rooftop looking at details on the horizon and immediately focusing on a handheld card with a parrot and cage, trying to get the parrot into the cage. This was much better than foot drill. However, our corporal wanted us to train to do what was called continuity drill. After one command 'Flight' we started by coming to attention, then a smart left turn and march for 20 yards or so, then about-turn and do all the drills like an open order march, slow march, change step. This was all done by counting silently and lasted about ten minutes. The corporal said if we did it correctly on the day of the visit of Air Commodore Critchley, the CO (Commanding Officer) of aircrew training, he would get his third stripe and become sergeant. He then said if we mess up "I'll make your life hell!" Actually, he was one of the best NCOs (Non-Commissioned Officers), some of whom could be horrible.

After our reception at ACRC, we were posted to a toughening up course in Filey, North Yorkshire. After our arrival, we were shown to a large shed, where at one end there was a large pile of used army boots, they were not even in pairs. We had to grab a left-hand and a right-hand boot something like a fit and that was ours for the next three weeks. I was in a room in a small hotel on the seafront, sharing with eight others, crammed in a bit. The first morning at 6 am, the corporal in charge came in yelling "everybody outside in PT kit and boots on". PT (Physical Training) meant we had to do a cross country run, it was horrible and I'd got blisters on my feet. This was drill every morning but I was very lucky, one of the guys in our room was a very experienced and interesting man. His name was Roger Morelle. He had an Irish mother and a French father and he had lived most of his life in France. He joined the RAF as a boy entrant and his last job before he re-mustered was to operate a drogue towed by a plane, for trainee fighter pilots to fire at. He said we got nearly as many bullets in the towing plane and he decided that he'd be better off firing the bullets! After the first morning, he got me to one side and said "I have done a little 'recce and we no more nasty runs. I 'av found a way into de loft here and de corporal when he comes in every morning he does not do a roll call, but dashes into every room to ensure it is empty. You and I will go up in de loft 20 minutes before he come in and then come down 20 minutes after all is quiet! Then we go into de little town and 'av coffee. We must be very smart, well-polished buttons, shoes polished up and we

35

march round in step, arms swinging and if we meet officer, we give smart salute". When this came about I was ready to dive into the nearest side street, but Roger said "Off we go marching past de biggest hotel which is HQ". and so we did. In three weeks, we were never stopped, but once I did a silly thing. There was a man in uniform coming the other way and I gave him a smart salute - he was a coastguard! I learned a lot from Roger over the next few months, for instance, if you are on a railway station platform when you should not be and you see a couple of military police don't try to escape, but go up to them and say something like "My watch has stopped, could you tell me the correct time please?"

After Filey, we were posted to a camp near Ludlow. A very basic experience with open-air latrines and smallish, round tents housing six of us each, where it paid to be the last one to bed so that your feet were top of the pile! Whilst there we were given a small chit, which gave us a list of ITWs (Initial Training Wings). Nearly all of these were seaside towns, usually large hotels and spread over the country from Torquay to St Andrews. I knew there were three ITWs in Scarborough, only about 10 miles from home so I put in a preference for Scarborough. Of the lads in our tent, one lad was a Scot, so he chose St Andrews. The result was, five of us went to St Andrews and the Scot went to Scarborough. A lesson learnt, they didn't want us to be near mummy and daddy!

After a dreadfully long journey, we de-trained at St Andrews, weary with full kit, full pack, kit tag, tin helmet and all. We were marched to our hotel. One lad meekly asked the sergeant in charge a civil question and the sergeant yelled "Stand to attention when you speak to me laddie", a taste of the strong discipline we were to endure during ITW. About twelve weeks of ground study covering maths, science, theory of flight, all essential subjects, including the rectification of the various causes of stoppage of the Browning machine guns. I was at a big disadvantage, especially in maths, when the instructor would say "You will remember this from your school days", things which I had never heard of. Luckily there were one or two lads who helped me when this was a problem. One thing I remember when we were learning to send and receive Morse code by Aldis lamp, we were on the famous golf course there, receiving signals from the clubhouse. Some of the lads were playing pitch and toss in the bunkers!

There was a great comradeship amongst us. After our time there, the exam results on all the various subjects came through. Less than 50% passed, the others that failed were sent to train as Air Gunners, Wireless Operator etc.

Life Number 3 - Even More Water!

From St Andrews, we were sent to nearby Scone airfield, where we would get our first initiation of flying. About half of us had never been airborne before, so this felt as if we were really on our way. The aeroplane we were to have our first flying lessons in was the de Havilland Tiger Moth, a descendant of the planes used by early record-breaking flights around the globe. A lovely little plane, which didn't feel so little the first time we approached it. This was known as a grading school, where we would be assessed as to our ability to learn and it usually meant an average of 10 hours before candidates were allowed to go solo. One or two lads who had maybe some experience as Air Training Corps Cadets went solo after seven or eight hours tuition, but I had got to 10 hours and my instructor had not suggested to me that I should have a go, so I plucked up courage and asked him if he would consider allowing me to go solo. He looked me up and down and said "OK, get your kit on, I'll see you outside in five minutes".

He was a good instructor, a man of few words, but very thorough. We did a couple of circuits and I made two reasonable landings. He climbed out of his cockpit and said "Off you go then, but don't bend this thing, we need 'em badly". I taxied out, opened the throttle and took off. As I was climbing up I suddenly felt apprehensive, what have I done? Then I thought just do everything as I have been taught. I made another decent, but not perfect landing and felt happy, however going solo was no guarantee that you had passed. There were three possibilities; you could be graded as pilot, navigator or air bomber, depending on your flying ability, ground subjects and your temperament.

We were all given a week's leave and told to report to Heaton Park, Manchester and we would not know our future training until then. Heaton Park was a huge area with paths around shrubbery and with a huge natural amphitheatre and bandstand below. The next day we were all assembled around this area with many others from different grading schools. A small team of men were on the bandstand calling out names and numbers, with the letters 'P', 'N' or 'B' according to your grading; pilot, navigator or air bomber. After hours of this, it finally came to my name and much to my relief it was 'P'. I had some doubts because I'd had to ask if I could go solo and worried if that had maybe gone against me.

After a couple of days, we were marched to a clothing store and given khaki shorts, etc., which we thought meant we would be going to Rhodesia, but at the last minute we were back, exchanging our tropical kit for heavy battledress and caps with ear flaps, so it was to be Canada.

We were entrained up to the Clyde and anchored there was a huge liner, not quite as big as the Queen Mary, but pretty big, the Empress of Japan, which was hurriedly renamed after Pearl Harbour as the Empress of Scotland. By this time it was dark and we were ferried out in smaller boats and had to climb up the side up a steel runged fixed ladder. It seemed like climbing up a mountain but eventually we made it up onto the deck. We were directed down endless stairs to a huge area, probably the luggage hold, way down below the waterline. It was just a massive area, empty except for piles of hammocks and rows and rows of hooks in the ceiling. There was a bit of a scramble to bag a hammock and, if possible, near the stairways, one leading down and the other to go up. The rows were so close together and the pairs of hooks in the ceiling so close that it was joked that if one person turned over in the night everyone in that row would have to do so! Having recently seen an engraving of the shocking plan to accommodate the maximum number of unfortunate slaves in a vessel it was not unlike the conditions down there. We estimated that there were nearly 800 of us and I remember one lad, on the first night sitting on a folded hammock in tears because he could not find any spare hooks, we were so crammed in.

We were allowed to go up on deck during the daytime. The facilities for toilet and ablutions were very basic, probably the crew's quarters and for a simple country lad like me it was a bit of a shock to see a row of doors with on one a crude notice which read "Ratings with crabs use this bog" and some wag had scrolled on the door "It's no use standing on the seat, the crabs in here can jump six feet".

We left the Clyde in the middle of the night and next morning when we were allowed on the lower deck we were clear of land, heading for Halifax in Nova Scotia. We had been at sea for a couple of days and were wandering around the deck on a cold bleak rather wet afternoon when one of the lads suddenly said "There's a periscope". We said "don't be daft", but looked and there it was, abeam of us and close enough for us to seemingly be looking down on it. It was so close that we reckon that he would have about a 60° angle to aim at and could not have missed with a torpedo. At that moment the ship did a massive turn to port, with the deck tilted so much that we were all thrown against the rails. Suddenly armed marines appeared to shepherd us all below decks and just before I disappeared off the deck I saw a huge net, probably a fishing net, which we had noticed earlier, where all the empty tea chests, packing cases and rotten vegetables, all of it was waste. It was kept in the net to avoid leaving a trail behind for the U-Boats to find, a practice that came from the old days of square-rigged ships used to avoid the risk of pirates tracking them. By doing this massive turn to port it put the U-Boat astern of us and dropping all this rubbish would help to block his sights and with luck may damage his periscope.

As we began to descend the dozens of stairs to our quarters there was a huge explosion and we all thought that we had been hit by a torpedo, however with armed marines urging you on you don't linger and we were soon way down below sea level in our quarters. We were wondering how long it would be before water came cascading down the stairways when one would be drowned like a rat in a trap. The ship was doing massive turns taking evasive action and we began to think that it was only a matter of time. I cannot describe the accumulative effect of nearly 800 souls feeling such fear and it went on all through the night. One lad had a battery-operated shaver and when he started to use it, a couple of guys jumped on him yelling "stop that", such was the nervous tension.

We think that there were two reasons why we were sent below so quickly. One was to clear the decks for action and the other was to lower the centre of gravity of the ship to make it more manoeuvrable. I never thought such a big ship could be flung about so much. We began to think that if we were shipping water badly the skipper would not be able to throw it about like that for a long time. It went on all night and the tension eased somewhat and we were trying to find an answer to why we were not apparently sinking. One guy suggested that the U-Boat had run out of torpedoes, but then he wouldn't have come in on the attack like he did, but kept out of sight and reported our position and heading to other U-Boats able to intercept us. The only theory that seemed logical was that someone had heard a rumour that a torpedo had been known to have gone into a steep dive out of control and passed under the target, but then what about the explosion we had heard?

Some years after the war had ended I read that French munitions workers, forced to produce torpedoes under strict Nazi control, were deliberately setting the controls of an average of 1 in 10 (they dare not do more in case of discovery) to go into a steep dive. Sadly, the Nazis did discover their actions and all the men in the factory were shot in front of their wives and families. I may only be sat writing this thanks to the brave actions of defiance by French patriots.

Fun and Games

When we were allowed back on deck the following mid-morning the sun was hot and the sea calm, one of the crew told us that the ship had been heading south all night and we were down by the Azores. It was only then that we discovered that the explosion was a 4" gun on our stern firing at the U-Boat. Now we were back on a westerly course, not north-west as we would have thought, and so, when we eventually saw land ahead we had no idea where we were, until, in the distance, in the twilight, we saw the illuminated Statue of Liberty! It was to be New York. The news of our escape must have been broadcast as we got a wonderful reception. Ships' sirens, horns and car hooters going and as the light faded all the lights in the city, with car headlights sweeping across, such a change after blackout Britain.

Spending the night on board ship, I felt so frustrated, thinking of all my jazz heroes playing in the clubs in the city and no way could I get to see and hear them. There was a small motorboat circling the ship looking out for guys, like me, tempted to jump ship. A modern version of the old oak battleships, with a rowing boat doing the same thing. No jazz in those days but many a temptation to sample other earthly delights!

For some reason, we were put on huge flat decked car ferries and crossed the river. Possibly to avoid approximately 1,500 of us being shepherded through the busiest part of New York. With us packed onto the deck of one of those ferries we suddenly started to sing a tune that was popular at the time – the 'Ferry Boat Serenade'. I think that the relief of it all meant that we were singing so lustily that a couple of years later a Canadian RAF Sergeant told me how he was amazed at the racket that we made. I was able to tell him that I was part of it. We were then entrained and travelled up to Halifax. On small stations on the early part of our journey the platforms were crowded giving us the famous Churchill V salute. I'm afraid some of us were returning it with the upside-down version of it. Eventually, we arrived at Halifax and were to stay overnight. We were allowed out that evening, it was a lovely clear night. We didn't feel cold at all, but we were warned to wear our headgear with the ear flaps down, otherwise, we'd get frostbite. The atmosphere is so dry compared to Britain and when Canadian troops were sent to Britain they felt the cold very much more than we did in their country.

One of the first things one lad did was to find a music shop and buy a guitar and I a pair of drumsticks. Once aboard the train where we were to be for the next 2½ days, en route to Calgary, Alberta, we found we were in a compartment with two guys who were very good harmonica players. We started having a bash at various tunes, with me drumming on woodwork. Suddenly the door slid open and a black-uniformed attendant looked in, slid the door shut and disappeared. We thought we were going to get into trouble for making a racket, but then he reappeared with a brand new looking trombone and he said "Can I sit in with you guys?" He was a professional musician and was travelling from the East coast to a job in Vancouver. We had two or three really good sessions, he was such a good musician.

Although we were never stationed together as they were training as navigators we sometimes found ourselves at the same station overnight and I found that these two guys were absolutely brilliant on piano. I'd love to have heard them on two pianos and we really enjoyed ourselves. Months later when we arrived back in Britain, after qualifying, we found that we were together again in Harrogate at the Grand Hotel, the largest of several hotels receiving trainees from overseas.

As we passed through stations in Canada there were people on the platforms holding up notices with British towns, offering a welcome to any of us from these towns. Unfortunately, I contracted pharyngitis and on arrival at De Winton, a small town and airfield south of Calgary I was hospitalised for ten days. When fit to begin Elementary Flying Training, a course on Tiger Moths of normally six weeks, I had to pack it into just over four weeks of training.

The Canadian built Tiger Moths differed in three ways from the British ones. There was a cockpit cover to keep out the cold which could be covered over to do instrument flying. Our British one had a tail skid that helped to keep the plane from swinging on landing, a bit like a sea anchor on ships, the Canadian version had a small tail wheel instead. They also had a black ball in a slightly curved tube, replacing the British turn and bank indicator. This ball and tube was 20 times more sensitive than the British instrument, ensuring that you had the correct amount of banking for the degree of rudder you were using in the turn. I can still hear the instructor yelling "Watch the ball, watch the ball".

I got through the course successfully, but I was lucky to some extent because when I came to do a solo cross country exercise I was halfway through it when my engine spluttered and stopped. As it happened I had spotted an airfield which I could just manage to glide into. We didn't have radio but I was able to put the plane down in a corner, well away from the runways. It was found that my petrol tank was empty. Before I took off I had seen a petrol bowser filling up the line of Tiger Moths and mine was one of them. Now, one of the pre-flight checks is to ensure you have enough fuel for the journey. I am fairly sure that I had checked it and claimed to have done so, but I sometimes wonder if I had assumed it. However, by this time, I had learnt never to admit something if there is any doubt. What I didn't know then was that this airfield was Penhold, a Service Flying Training school flying Airspeed Oxford twin-engined planes, where I was destined to go.

It was around this time we were taking a bus ride into Calgary. When we got on we found the white people at the front and the Indian people at the back. We were tempted to go and sit with the Indians, but I thought if there is any trouble it would be the Indians who would be turned off the bus, so the two of us sat in the empty middle seats and hoped we had made the point.

At Penhold we were shown over an Oxford and given

the pilot's notes, which included pre-takeoff and pre-landing checks. This was in a hangar and I remember thinking that the Oxford looked very large after the good old Tiger Moths and on sitting in the pilot's seat a bit worrying that there was very little of the plane in front of you to get an appreciation of the plane's attitude. After a couple of weeks' instruction, we were sitting in the pupils' room one morning when an instructor came in and said "Is there anyone in here who would like to train on single-engined fighters?" A lot of hands went up, so he said to one of them "Here's a brush, go and do an offensive sweep in the instructor's room next door". This became a routine thing and we all had to do it, in turn, every morning before the instructor arrived. It involved little more than a quick sweep and emptying the ashtrays, but it gave us all an opportunity to grab a quick look at our instructor's notes. When it came to my turn I was rather shocked to see in my case, in capital letters 'STILL HOPING'. I was very upset and decided I would have to pull my finger out and as we say in Yorkshire – 'Shape up lad'. I think that this may have been a deliberate policy to get the message across to us pupils.

I was really very lucky to get a good instructor who very quietly but firmly put me right. One of my pals had the opposite, a guy who yelled and swore at his pupils and my pal failed to make the grade, as I'm sure I would have if I'd had him as my instructor. I had him once on our first attempt at close formation flying. He would put the plane close in and then shout "You have control". I would generally ease out a little as I found it very difficult. If you are losing ground with the others and open the throttle a bit more, nothing seems to happen at first and you seem to be losing more ground, suddenly you start to catch up and you close the throttles but you keep on catching up. You need to anticipate and it's not easy, especially when you have this guy yelling in your ear "You bloody ham-fisted fool". I had him once in a night flying practice in daytime. This was achieved by the pupil wearing very dark goggles, to give the equivalent of night vision, just enough to see the runway lights which were put on for the exercise. I was making a real pig's ear of it, with two very bumpy landings. The instructor yelled out to me, in words which I wouldn't dream of repeating here, to the effect that "Would you please remove those perishing goggles and attempt to land this illegitimate aeroplane in some sort of fashion which would not reduce this blessed thing to a heap of something matchwood and would not leave us looking like some sort of potted meat!" When I removed the goggles I found that they were completely fogged up inside, not obvious till then, with them being so dark.

I had one good piece of luck later. I was to act as navigator, with an instructor flying the plane. We were to do a three-legged cross country flight and we were not given a wind direction or force at briefing, we had to find our own wind by using a three drift method once airborne. There was an instrument and a small window in the floor to get the drift, the difference between the heading of the plane and the actual path over the ground. You take the drift on three different headings and then calculate the wind speed and direction. You can then give the pilot the correct course to fly, having also taken into account the variation due to magnetic north shown on the compass being different to the true north. Also, the deviation which is due to the presence of metallic parts of the aircraft itself. Having done all this I gave the pilot the course to steer on the first leg and we hit the first point spot on. On the second leg, the pilot asked me if I wanted to change the new heading. I said no, I was quite happy with things. We made the second point OK and then turned for home. Again he asked me if I wanted to make any alteration. I said no. Eventually the airfield came into sight and I still said no changes were needed. We flew right over the control tower and the pilot said "We could have bombed it, you were spot on". In his report he put 'superlative navigating'. However, I was not able to boast about it because I did not know how to pronounce the word!

Later, when we had radio and we were able to communicate with the control tower other pupils said "You sound half asleep when you talk on the radio". I guess that was because I was trying to lose my broad Yorkshire accent.

One exercise we had to do was to talk continuously for a set time so that ground control points could get a fix and give us our position. The recommended practice was to count up to ten and then back to zero. Some of us thought that was a bit boring and as it was always a WAAF (Women's Auxiliary Air Force) on the receiving end we had other things to say. My one was "Little Jack Horner sat in a corner eating his Christmas pud. A girl came by and gave him the eye. Did he? Would you? I would". It never seemed to impress any of the WAAFs though.

The rest of the training on the Oxfords went reasonably well and about 50% of us received our wings.

Gaining my Wings 1943

After the presentation, we were given a week's leave and on a previous 48 hour pass my pal and I hitchhiked up to Edmonton. We were given a lift by an American businessman who told us that when we were given a longer leave we were welcome to stay at his home in LA. However, we found that we were to report to an airfield on Prince Edward Island off the east coast in a week's time, there was no way we could get to LA. Instead, I remembered as quite a young kid, playing with a little girl in our little village of Foxholes. She was visiting relatives with her parents and the family had given me their address in Winnipeg in case I ever got to Canada. We decided that we could break our train journey and spend a couple of days there. Then we could catch a train carrying the rest of the guys.

During our training we were told that the lads with the best results for both flying and ground subjects (i.e. navigation, etc.) would get the best choice of which type of plane we could move on to, but in the end, everyone was posted to Coastal Command, such was the dire threat posed by the enemy U-Boats. After the war ended we found that at its worst a fifth of the Merchant Navy was lost in one month and apparently, the Churchill memoirs revealed that, worried as he had been about the outcome of the Battle of Britain, he was even more worried about

56

the Battle of the Atlantic.

We arrived in Winnipeg, booked in a hotel and got a taxi out to where they lived. However, after explaining who we were, we found the girl was having her 21st birthday party, so we said we would call again the next day. The parents would have none of it, they said "You are staying right here" and when we told them we were booked into a hotel they said "Jump into the car, we'll go and fetch your luggage" and told Anne to get on the phone and get two more girls to the party. Such a wonderful reception and we had two great days there. Then back to the station to pick up the train for the rest of the journey.

This time there was no music, but a different way to relieve the monotony of the days on board. We found that there were two carriages of Canadian girls who had volunteered to join the Canadian Women's Auxiliary Air Force with one lady sergeant in charge. It happened that the dining car was situated so that we had to pass through the two carriages of Canadian beauties. Of course we were tending to dally and chat up these girls, but the sergeant kept waving us on, saying "These two carriages are out of bounds to you lot so get on through, no fraternising". The next day, because we were to travel over quite hilly terrain the train was split into two halves. As luck would have it one carriage full of girls was on one train, with the sergeant on board and the other train, which we were on, had the carriage full of girls with no supervision! Obviously, we were over the moon and that evening we spent most of the evening enjoying the girls' company. My partner was happy to have a bit of heavy petting, but quite definitely no more than that, so I eventually crawled back to my carriage, thinking enviously of the three or four lads who seemed to have got lucky! However, the luck was on my side as, at a brief stop at a small station Royal Canadian Air Force Military Police boarded the train and the lads in the wrong carriage were put on a charge of serious misconduct.

When we arrived at the airfield on Prince Edward Island we were told we would be on long-range night patrol and convoy or single ship escort, just about the most boring flying job we could have, but essential. This involved more navigational problems because we were not going to find a static target, but one where the ship or ships were moving. We knew roughly where they should be by the time we reached them after maybe three or four hours of flying but as we knew all too well after our experience on the way over to Halifax, there was a circle of uncertainty where the ship might be and there was strict radio or WT (Wireless Telegraphy) silence to avoid giving away the ship's position.

Our course there was to work with trainee navigators and there were civilian pilots to do the actual flying. The planes were Avro Ansons and they were a similar size to the Oxfords and far more stable and easier to fly, but less fun! We also had to learn ship recognition and I remember the instructor using the phrase 'Stick stack, stack stick' to define a ship - a mast, two funnels and a mast. A quick way to describe the different layout of the vessels.

On a ground navigation test, I finished second after a navigator and ahead of all the other navigators. I seemed to be good at something at last! But then I found that in the air over the rather choppy Gulf of St Lawrence and bumpy flying, I got my first and thankfully only bout of air sickness. Bending over the navigator's bench made it worse and on one occasion the staff pilot let me take over the controls, when I was OK, no problems at all. Maybe it was for the best as I didn't want to be kept on there as an instructor.

After the course there was an opportunity to train on American Catalina flying boats. One guy went there to Pensacola in Florida and when I met up with him about a year later he told me he had a great time there. The American people were very hospitable and once he was invited to a rather posh charity ball. He was dancing with a very charming young lady who, in the middle of the dance asked him "Do you shag?" Before he could think of a suitable reply she started to demonstrate the steps on the dance floor! It was the latest dance craze in the US. I don't think it ever got over the pond to Britain, which is perhaps just as well.

We returned to Britain on the Mauretania, again without naval escort. This time our crossing was without incident and we arrived back, to be entrained to Harrogate which was the town where overseas trained aircrew were stationed until the next stage of training. A lot of the hotels were used and we were in the largest, the Grand Hotel. As further training was behind schedule, after a long spell of bad weather, we were sent on a three week toughening up course in Whitley Bay, again with the RAF Regiment.

On our first day, we were marched to a small theatre and on the stage was a tough-looking RAF Regiment WO (Warrant Officer). He was to teach us unarmed combat, in case we were downed over enemy territory. After some blood-curdling descriptions of how to prevent an enemy from shouting for help, etc., he produced a piece of wood about 15 inches long and called up one of the lads onto the stage saying "This is a knife, attack me with it". The poor lad ended up on the floor yelling in pain and it was obvious that this WO was a sadistic devil, not content with demonstrating, but had to inflict pain as well. I, being tall, was trying to avoid his attention by squatting down in my seat and luckily for me he didn't call me up. There was one lad who came from the Gorbals district of Glasgow, who approached the WO in a low crouch with the 'knife' low down but he still ended up on the floor yelling in agony.

My pal and I found out that as an alternative to this we could take boxing lessons from a Corporal Phillips and, on the premise that anything would be better than more horror from the WO, we went and enrolled for the boxing training. It was in a gym with a proper raised boxing ring and we found Corporal Phillips to be a really enthusiastic teacher. If you forgot to keep your chin tucked in he would give you a light tap and if you still forgot another slightly harder tap, but not too hard. He taught us how to move, depending on whether your opponent was conventional, or a southpaw i.e. a guy who leads with his right hand. He told us that if we wanted more training he would be there every evening and as we had become quite keen we often would go in the evening.

One night I was in the ring with Corporal Phillips when he suddenly stopped and said "It's OK he won't hurt you, he just wants to get a bit of weight off". I turned to see this huge guy, about 6ft 8in tall and wide enough to have to go sideways through a barn door. He was wearing a black tracksuit, the first I'd ever seen and he came in, snorting and dancing making the ring shake, or was it my knees knocking? He didn't really hurt me but he frightened me to death. I found out later he was an ex-Golden Glove winner, the amateur heavyweight champion of the world! He was an officer in the RAF Regiment and once took us to practice grenade throwing. He could throw a grenade with a flick of the wrist further than we could in the conventional way. It didn't put us off going for more boxing lessons and although I was a bit too skinny to be a real boxer I remembered my dad telling us about a skinny lad who looked quite pale, almost unwell, but he made up for this by his ring craft, the great Jimmy Wilde. After the war Corporal Phillips became well known as Al Phillips, probably the most well-known British trainer of the time. He trained two British heavyweight champions. I think it was Bruce Woodcock and maybe Brian London if memory serves me right.

After the course finished we were sent to Desford, near Leicester, to fly Tiger Moths again, to practice map reading, a very good idea because map reading in Britain is completely different to Canada which has wide-open spaces. If you saw a railway crossing a river you knew exactly where you were, but in Britain, it is completely different, there is such a myriad of woods, rivers and railways.

One day on a map reading exercise I decided to look for Donnington Park, the car racing circuit Alan and I had visited on our cycling tour. I found it and did a low flying circuit of the track. It was much changed, being used as an army depot with trucks all over the place. Then I decided to head roughly back to Desford but did a bit of low flying along the River Trent. It was fine until I came across a line of electricity pylons and too late I realised that the two pylons carrying the cables across the river were much higher than the rest. It was too late to climb above the cables so I had to dive underneath them, hoping that no one had been able to read my number. It was a bit like learner drivers having got rid of the L plates and thinking they know it all, but are not as experienced as they thought they were.

Another naughty thing we did was to orbit a small

lake about 10 miles from the airfield. If we saw another Tiger Moth with only one occupant it was going to be one of us and not a pupil having his first flying lessons as we had done months before. We would then engage in a furious dog fight which, with Tiger Moth biplanes, was more like a WW1 dog fight than WW2. Nevertheless, I managed to have a semi-blackout after a very tight manoeuvre, everything went grey momentarily. This went on until one of our lads took part, but was thoroughly beaten up by his opponent. Then after landing, the Chief Flying Instructor had us all in for a right bollocking. He had twigged what we'd been doing and had taken off on his own and caught us out. He was quite right to say that map reading could at some point be a lifesaver and say more misconduct would have severe consequences. As it happened three of our lads, who were already airborne throughout this were to be seen overhead flying in very close formation. We were all lucky to have saved our necks let alone severe consequences.

After two weeks we were back to Harrogate where I found I had been posted from the fifth floor at the Grand Hotel – to the third floor!

Although we were now senior NCOs by this time we

had to do some drilling as well as PT. I was the tallest of our flight and was made marker, this meant having to be on parade 10 minutes before the parade time and subject to a close inspection by the Station Warrant Officer. I didn't like this, so, when marching off my experience as a drummer came in handy, as I was able to lead but my steps were slightly offbeat, the corporal said "What's the matter with you, why can't you keep in step?" I replied "I don't know corporal, I'm doing my best". He said "You're no good" and told the next tallest lad to take the lead and put me at the rear. That was OK until we did an about-turn and I was now at the front. I forgot to do as I'd done before and marched in step. The corporal halted us and asked me how it was that I could march in step this way. I said "I don't know corporal" he replied "I think I do" giving me a hard look, but I got away with it. I think in a way they quite liked it if you showed some initiative and it proved to be very useful a little later on.

During the next week or two, most of our lot were posted to different airfields to do flying control duties. Why I had not been posted I'll never know. Instead I was put down for another three weeks with the RAF Regiment at Whitley Bay, so I requested a meeting with our CO and told him that I had already done one there and one at Filey. He agreed it was unfair and I suggested that I thought the ebony black scale models used for aircraft recognition would be better if they were painted in authentic camouflage or whatever was appropriate. He agreed and gave me a pass to use in the town and a small sum for expenses. I carried this out, but have to admit that I attended a piano recital and sometimes I would have a bath and get ready for a night out.

During this time there was a dance in the ballroom of the Grand Hotel, with the station band playing. Much to my delight, I found that my two pianist friends had also come back from Canada and were in Harrogate waiting to move on as I was. At the interval they asked the pianist if they could have a play and were given the OK so I asked the drummer if I could go on the drums, he said I could, the guitarist also appeared and during our stint an American trainee appeared with his trumpet and we had a right old jam session. The dancers all came around the bandstand and when that happens you know you are doing well. Goosebump time for me! We finished with a very up-tempo version of 'Sweet Georgia Brown' and as the station band reappeared I heard one of them say "At least they all finished together".

Afterwards, we were approached by the entertainment officer there, a B.C. Hilliam who had been one half of the well-known duo 'Flotsam and Jetsam'. He asked us if we would do a turn in a show he was getting together. Of course we said we would, but sadly we were all posted away before the show and we lost touch. I felt that they were good enough to go professional and kept a lookout after the war, but never found any trace of them.

One experience at Harrogate which I hated was a ruling that all Coastal Command aircrew must be able to swim at least five lengths of an average pool. I had to confess that I was a non-swimmer and it did not matter that I was already scared of going completely underwater. There was a flight of about 30 non-swimmers and after early morning parade, we were all marched off to do different activities. I was very scared when the corporal PT Instructor took us to the deep end of the pool and said "Everybody sink down to the bottom and the first one to come up, I will jump on him". I had to try and managed somehow not to get jumped on but it was hell! The next morning, after discreet enquiries, I found that the flight next to ours were marched off to a sports ground by a corporal PT Instructor named Sam Bartram and thanks to my being at the end of the flight I was able to slip off the back of the flight I was supposed to be with, the non-swimmers flight, and join on to the end of Sam Bartram's flight. He was ex-Charlton

Athletic and all he wanted was to have the lads shooting four or five footballs at him from all angles to help keep his eye in. He was reputed to be the best goalkeeper never to be capped for England. It was a much better thing for me than getting scared to death in the swimming pool, so I never did learn to swim!

Life Number 4 - A Close Shave

Eventually, I was posted to the next stage of flying and arrived at Wheaton Aston airfield, about 11 miles NW of Wolverhampton. This was AFU (Advanced Flying Unit) and we were told on arrival "OK you've got your wings, but we are going to make you into REAL pilots". We were back flying Oxfords, the twin-engined trainer and given much more training on the use of bomb sights, etc. By this time we knew we were going to Coastal Command and would be flying in all weather conditions, but I was hardly prepared for one incident. We were all pilots but were paired up to do night-time cross country exercises. To do it once as a pilot and once as a navigator with the same guy, with a Wireless Operator to make up a three-man crew. I was paired up with Jock, a nice enough lad, but getting a reputation as a budding alcoholic. When not flying a small group of us would cycle down to the nearest village pub and Jock had an ambition to get the publican drunk. Whoever was buying a round would ask the landlord to have one. Of course he didn't always, but he was a decent guy and he would put the money aside until there was enough to buy us all one on the house. The landlord and his wife got a bit worried about Jock and after closing time they would ask Jock to go through to their living quarters and have a coffee to sober him up a bit. This meant that we would all be settled back in our Nissen hut, which had two rows of beds and one coke stove in the middle. The drill was to choose a bed near, but not next to, the stove where you would be too hot, but not at the extreme ends of the hut where you would be frozen. We would all be settled down and asleep when Jock would arrive. He would be too drunk to remember which was his own bed and one night he was trying to get into my bed, saying "You're in my bloody bed, what are you doing in my bloody bed?" There was nothing for it but to go and kip down in his bed. But later, in the early hours, Jock would have to attend to a call of nature. There were no toilets handy, but a few bushes which offered a slight degree of privacy. Jock would then blunder his way back into the hut and this time find his own bed shouting "You're in my bloody bed again man, what the hell are you doing in my bed again!" There was nothing to do but retreat back to my own bed, trusting it was in a fit state to occupy. This happened once or twice more, but not to me again.

One day was a real beast of a day with pouring rain and very low cloud often right down to the deck as we called it. None of us were expecting flying to go ahead that evening, but to our amazement, at late afternoon briefing, we were told that flying was on and Jock and I were to do the cross country exercise again, this time with Jock as pilot. After the briefing, Jock came up to me and said "I never thought we would be flying tonight and I've had a wee drop or two". As soon as he got near to me I could smell his breath and I thought more like four or five! Much to my relief he asked "Would you fly the bloody thing tonight?" I quickly agreed, I'd done it the once as pilot with Jock navigating so I had a fair idea where we were going. It was the same three-legged cross country, the first leg to Chivenor in North Devon, where we had to overfly and contact them by radio to prove that we had found it. Then from there to Kidlington near Oxford and then the third leg back to base. We took off in foul conditions, got to Chivenor OK then set course for Kidlington. It was all blind flying with about 10/10 cloud right down to ground level. Along the second leg, I got a glimpse through the murk of an airfield using FIDO (two rows of strong burning flares down each side of the runway in an effort to disperse the fog). With more experience, I should have aborted the exercise and asked permission to land there, but at that moment we got a recall back to base at Wheaton Aston. We assumed that the weather must have improved there, so we set course for base. We still had no visibility at all, relying on instruments. Now if you are driving down a country lane without cat's eyes or a kerb in thick fog, it's possible to wonder if you have drifted over to the wrong side of the road, but that is on the one horizontal plane, whereas in an aircraft there is the uncertainty of the vertical as well when there is no visible horizon to go by.

We were OK until suddenly we got the audible warning signal of Birmingham Barrage Balloons ahead, the frequency of this was changed every two hours and we had the frequencies on a card issued just before take-off. We had to do a detour to avoid them but eventually got back on course. We arrived back to Wheaton Aston and were overflying at 4,000 ft when there was a whoosh and a huge orange flame shot up just in front of us. "Did you see that?", came a call from flying control. Jock replied "You nearly took our nose off with it". We then started to lose height using a system of blind landing, flying a kind of elongated figure of eight known as the Lorenz Beam Approach, a system of navigational aid originally developed by the Germans. This was before we had radar in aircraft and was a really clever adaptation of the Lorenz beam, designed to bring you down in a controlled way which would keep you from high ground, electricity cables, tall trees, etc., providing you kept strictly to the system. I had done it once on the ground in the Link Trainer, an early type of flight simulator, but never in the air. It was a method using two transmitters at the start of the runway. For clarity, for example, supposing the runway was directly East to West with one transmitter sending dots to the Northern sector over 182 degrees and the other one sending dashes over 182 degrees to the Southern sector, so that in line with the runway the dots and dashes merged into a single continuous note. You knew then that you were in line with the runway. Your compass could tell you which direction you were heading. There was also an outer marker beacon making a 'caw caw' sound and an inner marker beacon making a 'pip pip' sound. On your final approach, you should be at 700 ft for the outer and at the second one at 50 ft, when you could put on full landing flaps and close the throttles and hopefully pick up the first runway lights, even if you could only see one or two. It took about seven circuits of the figure of eight losing height all the time before we got down to the final one. I used a system of counting the seconds before each turn, a way an instructor had taught me by thinking 'a thousand and one, a thousand and two', etc. I had practised it so that I could count up to sixty to within an error of plus or minus one second. This was essential as I could keep my eye on the flying instruments and not needing to look at the clock.

All went to plan until the final descending turn to port to line up with the runway and land, still with virtually nil vision. Halfway through the final turn suddenly there was a reddish glow of a radial air-cooled engine and then a huge landing wheel descending on us and coming the opposite way! We expected the landing wheel to smash the cockpit and instantaneously I made a diving steep turn to port and the approaching plane made a climbing turn to his left, both being the only thing to do to avoid a head-on collision. Even so, I think it was a miracle that his landing wheel didn't take our fin and rudder off, it must have missed us by inches. Both of our evasive actions were the only way to avoid contact, but I think that mine, to do a violent dive and turn from 800 ft, which also took us out of our safety envelope was the riskiest thing.

As soon as I realised that we had not made contact I opened the throttles and started a climbing turn that I hoped would bring us back into the safety area and by this time we were well into the dash area. We circled round and eventually hit the continuous note, but went right through it into the dot area, so we were able to continue our descent. A quick change of direction got us back on the right line but this deviation from the correct routine meant that we had missed the outer marker beacon, but we continued to descend until we suddenly heard the inner beacon. This meant we were about 150 ft instead of 50 ft. I had had enough by this time and I'm not going back into that murk again with possibly another plane lurking about, so I closed the throttles, put on full landing flap and luckily spotted a glimmer of runway lights. With these weather conditions, there is very little wind to land into to slow down your ground speed and the plane seemed to want to float along before the wheels touched the ground and we must have been halfway down the runway. I had read about rally drivers doing cadence braking, stabbing the brake pedal and releasing before the wheels locked and I learned all about it in the next few seconds! In those days nearly all planes had a tailwheel and if you braked too hard the plane would flip over onto its back, not a pleasant thought if you are doing over 80mph. Even using the above system the tail came up a few times, we must have seemed a bit like a pied wagtail! We were still going too fast when the end of the runway came up. I managed to swing it round onto the perimeter track with the outer wing tip nearly touching the ground, we would have ground looped and crashed if it had and we rolled to a halt. Jock started to thump me on the back shouting "Great man, great!"

When we got up to the control tower the DFO (Duty

Flying Officer) and the rest of them looked pale and in shock. The DFO started to tell Jock off for doing steep turns close to the runway. Jock stood up to him and said "We should never have been flying tonight and it was madness to recall us back to conditions like this". It was then we realised why they were so pale, what we didn't know till then was that, after the sound of our engines died away as we were entering the last phase of our approach, they heard a loud crump and thought we had come to grief. Unfortunately, it was the Wellington bomber we had narrowly missed. In doing his climbing turn he had lost control and crashed, killing all six crew members. I felt bad about it, but we both did the only possible action to avoid a head-on collision, plus I thought I was taking the biggest risk. The Wellington airfield was really too close, only about five miles from ours. He was not near their circuit and may have been using an early type of radar. Nevertheless, a tragic outcome which I'll never forget.

Serious Stuff

As it happened we had just received news that Alan was posted missing and it was then that I started to hit the booze. I could not get it out of my mind that what if my parents had received a second telegram about me if I hadn't survived the previous night, both their children lost in two nights. One or two beers wasn't enough. I had to get legless, but never when about to fly. I found out recently figures which were kept top secret at the time, that Bomber Command crews had only a 20% chance of surviving one tour of operations of 30 sorties (some did 33 or 34) and a shocking 2.5 % chance of completing a second tour.

At the end of this course I was being assessed by a Wingco (Wing Commander) who was an ex-Battle of Britain pilot, now doing instructing. All went OK until the end of the test, but as we prepared to join the circuit and land I banked to the right to check no other planes were coming in, he suddenly shouted "I have control" and banked much more severely, saying "You didn't check for other aircraft". I was 100% sure I had done so and there were no other planes in sight. I argued with him and failed to concentrate on the final approach and landing. It wasn't too bad, but in his report he put "Failed to keep a good lookout for other aircraft when airborne and a very poor landing". Later my regular instructor asked "What was that all about?" I gave him my version of events and he came with me to do two take-offs and landings, which were fine, but of course that comment was on the Wingco's report which was not good.

Some months later we heard that the Wingco had walked into the path of a taxiing Spitfire at a fighter station and was killed. It was well known that Spitfire and Hurricane pilots cannot see directly in front of them because of the huge engine and they taxied in a zig-zag fashion, but it was always the responsibility of the people on the ground to keep well clear of them.

At the end of the course we were posted to Operational Training Units and my posting was to Silloth, an airfield on the southern side of the Solway Firth. One of the first problems for me was an exercise where we were all in an indoor swimming pool, in nearby Carlisle, where a six-seater dinghy was floating upside down and each one of us had to go in and right the dinghy. So this was no good to me as I still could not swim and the drill was to put your feet into the rope looped around the thing, grab hold of ropes opposite and kick and pull at the same time. This meant you almost always ended up underneath the damn thing. I panicked a bit, but had a bright idea, there was a lad about the same build and hair colouring. I knew he was a chain smoker and we had got a free ration of 50 fags per week, so as he was quite a long way alphabetically from me, I said to him "I'll give you 50 fags if you go in twice, once for me and then go in again when you are called." As his name was Webb we were spaced well apart so we got away with it. Ironically I was to spend the rest of the European war flying out into the North Atlantic.

It was at Silloth that we were to be crewed up and there was a clever way in which this was done. There were 60 of us together in a large room, with a long bar and as much free drink as you wanted. Of these 60 men, ten were pilots who had completed half a tour of operations as second-pilots in modified Wellington planes, adapted to do long patrols of up to 11 hours, therefore needing two pilots. The rest of us were 10 pilots straight from training, 10 navigators straight from training and 30 others who would spend 20 minutes on the radar, 20 minutes on WT and 20 minutes in the rear turret, all from training. This meant there was never a completely green crew going into operations, as pilots with a full tour ended their tour, we would have completed half a tour and we would get a new second-pilot. It was thought that 20 minutes on the radar was the maximum before you would lose concentration, so the members were all trained to use radar, WT and rear gunnery. As the afternoon wore on we gradually got together to make ten crews, after much checking on personality, temperament, etc. All very informal and my first-pilot later told me that as I was 6 ft 2½ inches tall and he was over 6 ft tall we could change over without any adjustment of controls or seat! He was a great guy though and a very good first-pilot. One of the first tips he gave me was, if you are going for a booze-up, get your round in early, as most groups get larger as the night goes on!

Also in our crew were two lads who were very hard done by. They had trained and qualified as navigator wireless operators and would have expected to go on Mosquito or Beaufighters, but had then been posted to train as radar operators and rear gunners, such was the necessity to contain the U-Boat menace. The other crew member was already a long-serving Warrant Officer with a long history of ground duties who had re-mustered to train as rear gunner having then done the radar and WT courses. Jock had the advantage that everywhere we landed he would know someone there, usually someone behind the bar in the sergeant's mess, where he was able to negotiate some decent beer at a decent price to take back to base, no questions of course! The beer at RAF Benbecula was horrible and at a progress meeting someone suggested we should get a vet to examine the horse!

When we were getting crewed up two of the crew said "Doesn't he look like Pete" and from then on I was known as Pete, but I didn't mind. It could have been quite useful if some girl came looking for me for retribution she would be asking for Brian and I was known as Pete. Actually, we all had names that were very short to pronounce and also distinctive. There was Bob, Brad, Pete, Mick, Chas and Jock. Useful in an emergency when communications had to be quick and unmistakable. We all got on well together. One of our early exercises was to find an isolated rock in the Western Approaches, which is better known as Rockall these days, from the weather forecast. We had a different name for it! We had to photograph it to prove we had found it. These photos were worth a couple of packets of fags from frustrated crews who hadn't found it. Our first attempt to use radar at night proved to be a bit embarrassing. There was a small MTB (Motor Torpedo Boat) cruising round in a large designated area in the Irish Sea and we had to find it and do a mock attack with smoke bombs if we found it. This area was not marked out in any way and so its edges were not clearly defined. Because the U-Boats were able to crash-dive pretty quickly we had to fly at only 800 ft in order to get down low enough, in the time, to drop our depth charges. The drill was that if the radar operator got a blip on his screen he could home us on to it, losing height as we went until, at a range of ¾ of a mile at 200 ft we could switch on our Leigh light, a small powerful beam like a searchlight and if the last call from the radar operator was ¾ mile 2° port the light operator would set the light to 2° port and the right elevation to illuminate the target. It meant that we could do effective patrols and ship escorts at night as well as in daylight. We had searched for the MTB for an hour with no success. The radar operators needed a lot of experience and the early radar was not as clear as it became later. At the end of our hour we were just about to give up and head back to base when the radar operator shouted "I've got a blip!" He homed us on to it and at three-quarters of a mile we put the light on. We found we had illuminated a huge cruiser and could see his guns following us. "Light off", was the call and we fired off the Very cartridge which showed the colours of the day, which changed every two hours or so and luckily they didn't

82

blow us to bits. I guess that when they picked us up on their radar we would be showing a blip with a slight L shape to it. This was known as IFF (Identification Friend or Foe) and was a clever modification from our very wonderful radar scientists. In the early stage of WW2, there were examples where both sides attacked their own forces until IFF came along. There was a bit of a stink about our incident. We claimed that we were in our designated area and the Navy said not. We were probably right on the edge. This was not counted as Life Number 5 but just an incident along with many that occurred.

Life Number 5 - With No Undercarriage

Life Number 5 came a bit later in the course when we had to find a target in the Irish Sea, this time in daylight and drop six smoke bombs. There were two points on the Welsh coast from which we could take angles and check how near we were and photos by us to show how accurate our bombs had been, on this very small target. I was flying out to the target when one of the crew shouted "We have got a large oil leak on the port engine" and suddenly the engine began to vibrate massively and I had to switch it off and feather the propeller to reduce air resistance. We then found that the starboard engine was not producing enough power to keep us in level flight, so we asked flying control if we could abort and return to base. I had to stay on the controls as it would have been dangerous to change seats, due to the amount of force needed on the rudder bar to retain control and I asked flying control if we could come straight in without doing a circuit. The WAAF on the radio said we could and that they would stack up the other aircraft at 1,000 ft intervals, as they still do today in emergencies. All went reasonably well but as the port engine operated the oil

84

pumps which in turn powered the undercarriage and landing flaps we would have to use the emergency hand pumps. However when we found that didn't work either there was a huge problem. I radioed back to base that we would have to do a belly landing and we were told to land on the grass on the starboard side of 06 runway. As we approached we could see the fire tender and the blood wagon racing into place. We managed it reasonably well but in the excitement, I forgot two things: to jettison the smoke bombs and to switch my radio off transmit so that all the lurid language we used was transmitted back to base! As we slid to a halt with turf stacking up at a huge rate, inside the cockpit just right for a lawn, suddenly the smoke bombs went off and the plane filled up with thick black smoke. We thought that the whole lot was going to blow up in flames and almost before the plane came to a halt hatches flew open and six bodies were seen to race off in all directions. Luckily it didn't catch fire and the only damage to the Wellington was a bent propeller and the fabric on the underside of the fuselage was partially ripped off.

Loss and Gain

When we got up to the control tower the WAAF who had been on the radio started to tell me off for using foul language over the RT (Radio Transmission) but as a peace offering I had a spare ticket for a station dance in the largest hotel in Silloth. Even so the dance floor was very small and tickets were in short supply, always useful to have a spare ticket. She agreed to go and we met outside the venue. All tickets had to be signed on the back and as she hadn't got a pen I lent her my Watermans special fountain pen, top range with a 100-year guarantee. The next morning I went to use my pen and it wasn't in my pocket. I remembered and thought 'that damn WAAF has still got my pen!' I dashed down to the WAAF quarters and asked one of the girls where would I find this girl. She said "you'd better hurry up" as she had volunteered to go to India and was to have a medical and get the necessary jabs. I managed to find her, got my pen back and another date to go to the cinema. To cut a long story short she cancelled her plans and within three months we were married! So she stayed in Britain and later I was posted to India and had my pen pinched out there.

Our Wedding January 1945

The rest of the crew were not happy at my upsetting the drinking school and I'm sure they were lacing my beer with something stronger. I remember one night I left early to meet Emma who was coming off duty on flying control at midnight. I got there early and was able to hold on to the control tower which seemed to be swaying about a bit. When Emma came downstairs and met me I left hold of the control tower and promptly fell over! She wasn't at all pleased!

We were flying Wellingtons with the more powerful 14-cylinder Hercules engines as we needed more power. They were fitted with extra fuel tanks in the fuselage. I met an RAF fitter at a jazz weekend recently who said that the worst job he'd had was fitting extra tanks in Wellingtons until you could hardly move in them. I told him one of our crew, on seeing them for the first time said "It's a wonder they haven't filled the Elsan toilet with petrol!", but it increased the range we could fly. It meant that the wing loading was far higher than Barnes Wallis, the original designer, had envisioned and on take-off it needed a much longer run. We could be roaring down the runway thinking 'is it ever going to lift off?' When the weather was bad and often you couldn't see more than half the runway, it was a bit worrying. If you had a 'prang' with bombs on board there was a chance that if the bombs were not fused they may not go off, but with our load of 100 octane fuel it would go up, no question. But you couldn't leave a convoy out in the Atlantic unescorted just because of the weather, so we sometimes joked that we were flying when even the seagulls were on foot!

One particular day, when the runway in use had some high ground ahead and you had to start a gentle turn to port as soon as the wheels left the ground, we were relieved we were not flying as we had just finished a long night patrol. We were in our aircraft to test the RT system which had been giving trouble, so we could hear what was going on. A Wellington was sitting on the end of the runway waiting to take off on a convoy escort. You could only see about one-third of the runway. The pilot refused to take off until there was a little break in the conditions. He said that he would not risk the lives of his crew. The Flight Commander came racing down in his MG and ordered the pilot out, climbed into the cockpit and took off. It was a situation where we wouldn't leave a convoy without aerial escort although even today large airports would have been shut down. The poor lad was charged with LMF (Lack of Moral Fibre), stripped of his wings and rank and sent to a 'correction camp'. We used to say that in WW1 you were shot for cowardice, now it was LMF when you probably wished you had been shot before they had finished with you.

In all our operations we never saw a U-Boat, but our patrols kept them out of mischief. With a large convoy, even say with two destroyers or frigates their speed wasn't sufficient to give the convoy full cover. The U-Boats would wait till one had passed and then move in, but we at 200 mph could do a patrol that meant that if we didn't pick it up on one circuit we could do so next time round and with the Leigh light and radar we were just as efficient at night time when the U-Boats were more active.

Life Number 6 - Lazybones

We were able to help in bringing the shipping losses down from the horrifying fact of losing one-fifth of the Merchant Navy in one month, at that rate we would have lost the war. We also did single ship patrols and one of these was to meet the HMS Renown battleship in the Western Approaches and escort it to Scapa Flow. The weather was atrocious and a lot of the time we couldn't see the ship, but we had her on our radar.

It went OK and we left her at Scapa Flow. We decided that with the weather being so bad we had just enough petrol left to get to Benbecula by going around the Scottish and Hebridean coast rather than risk flying blind over the Scottish Highlands where all too many planes had come to grief. Brad, the navigator, had been working hard to calculate the running box patrol around the ship, so we told him to get his head down for a bit. We could pick up the coastline on the radar and I told the radar operator to keep a look out for the NW tip of the mainland so we should pick up the NW coastline of the Hebrides, after which we could turn more south to approach Benbecula from the sea to do our landing.

We were all tired by this time and I should have realised that we were heading slightly more South Westerly than the mainland heading. I kept asking the radar operator if he had picked up the Hebrides which we could not see visibly. Actually we had missed the NW tip of the mainland and were following the Hebridean coastline. I then realised we were not where we were thought to be and were heading out into the Atlantic! I shouted "Wake Brad up" and when Brad realised what we had done he gave me a course to turn to off the top of his head and then got a fix and his first estimate was only $2°$ from the right one. I went for the most economical cruising speed and gently down to about 100 ft to get the plane in its most efficient flying attitude. We knew the Wellington didn't ditch very well and so we were quite worried that our mistake could prove costly. We only just got home with the fuel tanks showing empty and as we taxied round first one engine cut and then so did the other - it was that close to a watery end[3].

---

[3] Wellingtons only had two engines.

Unemployed

Another less hazardous but more amusing episode happened a while earlier. We had an evening off and booked a Bed and Breakfast in Carlisle so we could get sloshed and didn't have to travel back to camp that evening. We were in a pub, one of a few and it was very crowded, the atmosphere was really bad, so much so that I suddenly decided I needed some fresh air. I went out of the front door and, in the black out, I walked bang into a lamp post. I remember the ground coming up to meet me, but nothing else until the lads awoke me with their laughter. I was fully dressed, with a head wound, the pillow was marked with blood and grime. They were laughing, I was not. How I found my way back to the Bed and Breakfast I will never know.

The next day we had an air test after our plane had been serviced. We were up in the control tower with about 20 minutes to go when I just keeled over, a case of delayed concussion. A few days later I was fit again and we had to do PT. The corporal PT Instructor, looking for an easy life, asked us if we would like to do press-ups or a game of football. We opted for football of course and we were split into two teams of 12 and it was virtually pilots vs navigators.

The guy who was to skipper my side asked me if I was any good. I said "Not really", so he put me in goal. One of our team said to me "You need to watch that navigator on the other team, he was a professional and played for Ashington", a small mining town near Newcastle. I said "No worry that's only a non-league team". I didn't know then of course that Ashington would produce the Charlton brothers and 'wor Jackie Milburn. This guy put two sizzlers past me, bottom left-hand corner and bottom right-hand corner, so our skipper took me out of goal and I found myself defending against this guy. He rattled me around the ankles a few times and I stupidly lost my temper. I thought the next time the ball goes near him I'll flatten him! So when that happened I went charging in, but he was too quick and left his foot behind, I tripped and went down. There was a crack and I had a dislocated shoulder. I was carted up to sick quarters and the MO (Medical Orderly) said "Not you again". He removed his shoe, put his foot under my armpit and jerked my shoulder back. I yelled out, but it was done. The MO said "You must keep your arm in a sling for a week, so obviously you can't fly with one arm, so I'll give you a chit to take to the CO and he will give you a week's leave". When I got to see the CO he said OK and I said "With respect sir, the crew say they don't want to fly with anyone else". He said "They bloody well will if I say so, but there are no spare pilots and they would only make a nuisance of themselves", so he wrote them a pass too. I was very popular with the lads!

That evening I was on the platform in Carlisle station when my train arrived. There was a big crush to get on the train, even for a place in the corridor but suddenly a guy shouted "Make way for the RAF lad" and there was I, face all colours of the rainbow, arm in a sling and of course showing my pilot's wings. The crowd all parted and let me get on board. I was standing in the corridor when a guy inside a compartment came out and said "Have a seat lad – rough time?" I nodded and smiled, but my smile was really what they would have done if I had explained how I'd got into this state! I could imagine the guy who had given me his seat would be telling his family of his good deed!

After the war, I was watching an episode of 'This is Your Life' on TV. The subject that evening was that wonderful footballer Stanley Matthews and his famous effort in the 1953 Cup Final when his side, Blackpool were losing 3 – 1 with about 25 minutes to go. Stanley went mad with terrific runs down the right wing, weaving his way past defenders and putting a cross in for one of his team to score. Result in the last minute 3 – 4! It was always called the Matthews Cup Final, but Stanley said it should have been known as the Morty's Cup Final because his teammate Morty scored the first three goals.

Then in walked Morty (Stan Mortensen) and as soon as I saw him I realised that he was my opponent when I dislocated my shoulder. He is still the only man to have scored a hat trick in an FA Cup final at Wembley and had also played for both England and Wales in the same match, a wartime game when Wales had a man hurt and Morty played for them in the second half.

Stanley Matthews said Morty might have scored four because when he put in the fourth cross he thought – where has Morty gone? Morty by this time had two defenders marking him, so he went to the far post taking the two defenders with him, allowing his Blackpool teammate Perry to score the winner.

Morty had a horrible incident in a Wellington when they hit a mountain in the Scottish highlands. Morty was the only survivor having a fractured skull, which put an end to his flying career in the RAF, but it obviously had not affected his football prowess post-war.

During the next year we used to get a bit fed up with the new marks of radar which were coming so often, but we had to get used to it. We didn't appreciate at the time how vital they were to keep ahead of the developments. I learnt much more about this after the war, as I will relate later. We owe a tremendous amount to the brilliant guys who worked night and day to develop new ideas. Two of the most well known were John Cockcroft and Bernard Lovell, both newly graduated and I believe Bernard Lovell had to be ordered to take a rest as he had been working all hours on a project until he was totally fatigued.

One of the last methods we were trained to use was a system called Sonobuoys. We would drop a pattern of four of these around a swirl left by a diving U-Boat. Each buoy, when it hit the water, shot out an underwater sea 'aerial' which picked up the sound of engines and the buoy also shot up an aerial transmitting the sound to us. Each one used a different frequency and when dropped in a diamond pattern around the suspected target, it was possible to plot the U-Boat and its heading. It was said to be accurate enough to damage a newly dived U-Boat and we were trained to recognise the different sounds made by different objects, even the sound of a whale.

By this time the enemy had produced U-Boats with a snorkel, a large tube divided in two, one half to act as exhaust and one half to supply fresh air so that the U-Boat could travel semi-submerged still using his diesel engines. These were much more difficult to spot, but again our radar was so much improved that we could still identify them, albeit at a shorter range.

I remember one much less technical but quite amusing thing. I was at Benbecula in the Outer Hebrides and I was trying to get a phone call to my parents who still lived in Foxholes on the Yorkshire Wolds. Their number was Thwing 17 and in those days you had a local exchange. The girl on the phone could not get Thwing right until I spelt it out for her. She suddenly said "Oh I get it, it don't mean a thing if it ain't got that Thwing!"

On VE Day (Victory in Europe 8 May 1945) and for a few days following we were escorting surrendered U-Boats to a port in Northern Ireland. I don't think the powers that be wanted any of them to sneak back to Germany. We were able to land and went inside a U-Boat. I could not get over the smell of diesel and foul air and the confined space inside, although they were roomier than our modified Wellingtons. I could not have done their job, but now we were unemployed!

Vickers Wellington GR Mark XIV, NB814 'RW-Q', of No.36 Squadron RAF shadowing a convoy of surrendered U-Boats off Northern Ireland 14 May 1945. Brian flew 'RW-Q' several times during April and May of that year. The bulbous chin housed the Air to Surface Vessel radar system used to locate U-Boats.

Life Number 7 - Hot Stuff

A few days later we pilots were posted away and on our last night in Benbecula we had a massive booze-up in the Sergeants' Mess. The sheep around there were running free and mostly kept away from us, but one old ram used to hang around and if you turned your back on him he would come and butt you. This last night some of the lads got him into the mess and he was charging about causing mayhem. Others got two geese and released them, they were flying from table to table sending the drinks all over the place. There was one lad burning his initials on to one of the roof timbers with his cigarette lighter. A bit of madness mixed with sadness as we were all going to be separated and for me, VE Day was the start of a whole lot of new problems.

All the NCO pilots, about 26 of us, were posted from Benbecula to Tarrant Rushton near Blandford, Dorset, which entailed a long boat and train journey. On the last leg, from London to Blandford, we got wind of a rumour that we were to be second-pilots to new crews straight from training in Halifax four-engined bombers to fly out to the Far East[4]. In every case, we had more operational hours flying than they had total flying hours in training. We got together en route and one guy, a tough rugby-playing Welshman, said "If we all stick together and say that we would not do this, instead we would do a quick conversion course and go out with our own crews as we were all experienced first-pilots". He said they would have to listen to us and as he looked around he said "It's the quiet ones I'm worried about" looking at me (I was a relatively quiet one I guess). When we got to Tarrant Rushton we found it was all too true and the top people were ready for trouble. There was the Station Commander, a Group Captain, the Squadron Commander, a Wing Commander and the Adjutant. They interviewed us one at a time in alphabetical order and didn't allow the guys who had been interviewed back to see the rest of us. When it was my turn I said what we had all agreed and I was put in a small room on my own. After what seemed a lifetime I was called back in. I repeated what we'd all agreed to say. The Group Captain said "You are the only one", of course I didn't know if

---

[4] The Japanese continued fighting in the Pacific war even though the war in Europe was over at this time.

this was the case so I stood my ground. He then went on to say "I'll give you 20 seconds to agree to it and if you still don't, you will be sent to India under armed escort and you will be charged with attempting to create mutiny and you will be sent to a place where you will end up wishing you had never been born!" I knew well what that would mean, bad enough in this country, but in the extreme heat that would be intolerable, so I reluctantly agreed to go. I was sent over to sick quarters to get the necessary jabs and on the way I met the others coming back. I said to Taffy "What about the quiet ones?" He just shrugged and said "What could we do?" I had been the only one, talk about all for one and one for all!

We were to fly out in stages to India with no leave. As it happened the planes had been fitted with small turbine-like blades around the propeller spinners in an effort to improve cooling of the air-cooled radial engines, a copy of what the Germans had done on their FW 190 fighters. We either hadn't got our design or material correct and found that ours were breaking off and becoming embedded in the cylinder fins. Because of this delay, we were given a week's leave and during this leave, we found that Emma was pregnant. She came down to Blandford with me, staying in a hotel there and to complicate things she was threatening a miscarriage. We had to get a doctor and he saved the day by fitting a ring around the cervix. Although most of the country were still celebrating after VE Day, it was a very worrying time for us.

The young crew that I was crewed up with were OK but it was with a heavy heart that I started off on our first leg from Tarrant Rushton to Castel Benito in Tripoli. The next day we flew to Tel Aviv. The following day the next leg was to one of the hottest airfields, about on the borders of Iraq and Iran in a desert-like situation. On the trip from the plane, around 8 pm we were on an open truck and trying to duck out of the hot air stream. When I was unpacking, getting ready for bed I put a bar of chocolate on the window ledge, out of the sun. The next time I looked it was running down the wall. I found it too hot to sleep in bed and went into the Sergeants' Mess and sat under a fan suspended from the ceiling, sipping warm cherry brandy. It was so hot that flying began at daybreak and was suspended at 9am. Everyone took cover until flying re-started at 7 pm till 11 pm. The heat and conditions were so awful that the ground staff personnel did six months, after which it was thought that any longer would send them bonkers.

One night was enough for us and early next morning

we found, on pre-flight checks, we had a mag drop on one of the four engines. It was a 50/50 thing and we decided to go ahead and get out of Shaibah. There was a well-known song in the RAF 'Those Shaibah Blues'[5] and we certainly appreciated it. We were OK on take-off and our next destination was Karachi. We put the aircraft U/S (Unserviceable) at Karachi to get the mag drop looked at and had a day off. We planned to have a look at Karachi and before we left one of the old sweats at the airfield said "When 'ya get into town you will be spotted with your pink knees and brand new khaki uniform and you will be surrounded by kids wanting baksheesh, but when you do, just snarl at them, 'Jaiow'". He was right and within no time we had about 30 kids pestering us. We said Jaiow whereupon they all ran round us in a circle shouting "You bugger off, you bugger off!" we had no answer to that and so they got their baksheesh.

We flew on the following day to Raipur in the Central Provinces. It was just about as central as you get in India, very flat, hot and dusty with very little greenery. Our job was to train and tow gliders full of Ghurkha troops and

---

[5] 'Those Shaibah Blues' became an expression of home-sickness among airmen.

104

drop them behind enemy lines in Burma. As we approached the airfield we saw three wrecked gliders dotted around the area of the camp. We soon realised why. We had followed an American squadron and on trying to get a loaded glider off the ground our engines were overheating to the point where the needles on the instruments were going off the clock and we had no alternative but to cast off. We could just about get an empty glider off, but that was no use. It was then decided to pack the fuselage with armed Ghurkhas and their equipment and drop them by parachute. I didn't look forward to being shot down behind the Japanese lines, with very few places to make an emergency landing and we heard rumours of the horrible treatment of people taken prisoner by the Japs.

We had not finished the training when we heard the news that the 'Yanks' had dropped the first atomic bomb, followed by the second one, with the subsequent surrender by the Japanese[6]. I must admit a feeling of relief on my part and fed up that had it happened only a

---

[6] The cities of Hiroshima and Nagasaki were bombed on 6 and 9 August 1945, respectively. The Japanese surrendered on 15 August.

few weeks earlier we would not have been in India at all.

After this, we started doing a sort of delivery service across India and one of our jobs was to collect a load of tents from Nagpur, only about 100 miles away. Our living quarters were about a mile from the Control Tower and on briefing, I realised that I had forgotten my flying helmet. There was enough time to go back to get it and I was just going out of the door when I felt someone pluck my sleeve. It was an army glider pilot who was now redundant, one or two of them used to come to the briefing each morning in the hope of getting a flight as second-pilot. He asked me, having overheard what I was going to do, "Could I go in your place as I've got my gear here?" We asked my young first-pilot if he was OK with that and he said yes, it was only a short trip so I was able to go back to the billet and 'charp it off' which was the term for an hour or two on the bed.

After about 2½ hours I got up and saw a huge column of smoke coming from the airfield. I jumped on a truck that was going that way to find that on the return flight they had an engine failure on the port outer engine and had to shut it down. You had to really nurse those engines due to the extreme heat. Even when parked with covers over the cockpit when you entered them you could hardly touch the controls, they were so hot. Luckily the pilots sat on their parachutes which we brought with us, otherwise we joked that we would have had toasted testicles!

On coming into land the pilot found that another plane hadn't got clear of the runway, so he had to do an overshoot and go round again. No problem normally, but as he opened the throttles to climb away the other engine on the port side cut out, so he had power on the two starboard engines and none on the port side, which sent him out of control. The port wing hit the ground and spun the plane into a line of parked aircraft, the huge Halifaxes. It pushed the first one into the second and all three went up in flames. As the weather was so hot the crew were only wearing shorts, so no protection from the flames. Sadly two of them were killed, also a mechanic, working on the parked planes. The others were so badly burned it was awful and the first-pilot's face was so badly smashed up he needed his face wired up and a series of skin grafts which left him looking mask-like. The glider pilot had so many injuries the MO said that it was only the fact that he was built like a heavyweight boxer that had saved him. If he had not been so quick to pluck my sleeve I would have been in the plane and with a slim build, I'd have been a goner.

Cross Roads

As all the rest of the crew were in hospital I was without a crew. I still attended briefing every morning but was never called on to fly, which after what had just happened, I wasn't too worried about. One night I was visiting the lads in hospital on the camp when a huge flying beetle came zooming into the ward. It headed towards a lad who had been lying on his tummy for a few weeks as his back was so burned that you could see bits of his spine. As the beetle flew straight for him he yelled and then threw the sheet over himself, but the beetle was too quick and ended up under the sheet with him! For the first time in weeks he got out of bed and the beetle took off and started to fly around, going very close to the crew navigator. He was an ex-policeman who had been patrolling the docks area of Liverpool, a very tough area, but he was really bothered about all the tiny insects, such as mosquitoes and of course scorpions as we all were. He yelled "Do something", we didn't know if it was harmless or not so I rolled up a thick magazine and managed to hit the beetle as it flew towards him. Once on the floor, I crushed its head, about the size of a sixpence and I took it to the anteroom to go on display with the other little beauties.

One concession we had been given back at Tarrant Rushton, there was a possibility that we could in time be taking over as first-pilots and this eventually happened to me. I did a bit of flying on the 'bus route' as we called it and one of my last trips was to ferry army lads from Calcutta to Karachi where they would be flown back to Blighty in Avro Yorks, a conversion of the Lancaster to a passenger plane with decent seating. As the crew were walking towards the plane the army lads were already waiting there. We were carrying our parachutes and one of the army lads asked "Do we get parachutes?" "No" said one of our crew, a real joker from Hull. "What happens if something goes wrong?" asked the army lad and remember that these guys had been under terrible strain fighting in the jungle. Our joker replied "We just get out quick mate". The poor lads got together and said "We will not get on board unless we have parachutes as well". I had to reassure them by saying "The parachutes will be stowed at the back near the tail of the plane and you guys will be between the crew and the parachutes, you have my permission to 'scrag' them if they try to get past you, however I need to sit on mine" and showed them the metal box where my chute fitted into "but I won't fasten up the harness and nothing is going to go wrong". That way we got them on board, but next morning on Daily Routine Orders it stated that parachutes must be stored out of sight before the passengers get to the aircraft.

After my flying days were over I joined an increasing number of guys waiting to get home but quite rightly we had less of a priority and we would travel home by ship. It turned out to be a long wait and various means of relieving the monotony were employed. One small group of lads from the next hut had got hold of some RAF camera 5-inch film and put a small amount of it into an empty Shinio[7] tin which was tapered down into a small fillet. They put a pair of wings on to the tin and made a sloping wooden ramp as a launching pad. This worked very well but if they packed too much film into it, it would take off and fly, but then explode with a loud bang. One day this happened over an open touring car carrying a visiting high ranking official. Not the welcome he would be expecting. The launchpad was hurriedly put out of sight.

One of the lads in our hut had bought a couple of little

---

[7] Metal Polish

monkeys. We said he shouldn't encourage this trade, but he said they looked so sad he couldn't resist them. We all got to like them and see them playing happily outside the hut, but as the 'rocket men' started to set up their gear the monkeys would shoot inside our hut and you could see two little faces peering out of the window.

The lad who had bought the monkeys had been starting a medical career and been training about three months before he volunteered to join the RAF. He asked me if I'd like to go with him to Bombay once a week to the University there. The MO had arranged for medical trainees to continue their studies and as we had nothing to do in our spare time I agreed. It was a good idea that would solve the problem of what I would eventually do when demobbed. We got a whole week's work to do on the necessary subjects, Biology, Chemistry and even a bit of Latin, which was difficult for me as we didn't even do English properly at Foxholes School never mind languages.

We did this during the next six months and the MO there said that there would be such a shortage of doctors and dentists in Britain that we would be able to get grants to enable us to continue. When I wrote and told my parents of this they wrote back to tell me that our family doctor said "Tell him to do dentistry, the hours and the pay are better!"

One of the monkeys used to sit around a lot with its head in its paws and his owner decided that he probably had toothache. He was able to con the medical people to let him have a little chloroform. He soaked a handkerchief in chloroform and held it under the monkey's nose as it was asleep using the folded mosquito net as a hammock. The monkey's head seemed to drop a little and we thought it was working so that his teeth could be looked at. Suddenly the monkey gave a screech, leapt out of bed and shot through the open window and raced up to the top of a small tree chattering away, so he didn't get his dental inspection.

There was always a lot of kite hawks circling around (we had a slightly different name for them) and we would get a small scrap of meat to which we tied a very thin thread which had a paper glider fixed to the other end, hoping one of them would swoop down and tow the glider away. If we threw a piece with no thread they would have it in a flash, but never could we get one to tow the glider, even if we tried to cover the thread with dust. Once when I was Duty Officer for the day and was inspecting the airmen's mess at mealtime a lad was complaining bitterly. They had to collect their main meal and pudding and go to the next building, about two metres away, under a covered awning. As he was carrying his meal using both hands a kite hawk swooped down, grabbed his main course and sent his pudding flying. The staff refused to serve him a second meal but I managed to persuade them to let him have another.

Eventually, I was posted away to train as a Flying Control Officer. I was going to be sent to visit airfields in Calcutta, Delhi, Karachi and Bombay, before returning to Poona to take up flying control duties there. I knew I was going to be away from base for at least five weeks and letters from home would be following me around for some time. Just before I left I was relieved to find a signal for me. Two numbers, which each represented a phrase and the numbers meant 'Son born. All well'. I was so glad that I had got this the day before I left. After the five weeks, I got back to Poona, I got a letter from Emma direct to Poona saying that there is still a chance that our son may yet survive! I had no idea what the trouble was but obviously, it was extremely serious. I took the letter to the CO, the MO and the Padre asking for compassionate leave and of course the war was well and truly over by this time so they should have been sympathetic. I could not get leave and when I asked them why not, I was told "You haven't seen your son". I said "No but I have seen his mother, she was in a rented room in Leicester and will be beside herself with worry". But to no avail, I could not get leave.

As an alternative to a medical career, I had for a time considered staying in the RAF but now all I wanted was to get back to England as soon as possible. When I got the letters that had been chasing me around I found that Stuart was born with a weight of 8lb 6oz, but had Pyloric Stenosis and after every feed, he had projectile vomiting and was literally starving to death. Emma had Stuart in a private nursing home and they said "He's OK, he's just a greedy feeder". She then had two private doctors who failed to diagnose it. One of them suggested she may have been worried over me flying in India and it was upsetting her milk! He just lost weight, down to 5lb 8oz and seemed just skin and bone. At the last chance, she heard about a clinic specialising in child diseases and took him there. He was seen by an elderly doctor, who felt Stuart's tummy and said immediately what it was. He said the normal treatment in those days was to operate to relieve the overactive muscles that were not allowing food to pass further through the digestive system, but Stuart was too weak to be operated on. The only hope was to try a new drug, Emetrol which was ironically developed in Germany. He was injected about 15 minutes before a feed and the drug relaxed the muscles sufficiently to allow the milk through. The doctor warned that there was only a slim chance that it was not too late, but if he did survive he would see off the usual child complaints well and that proved to be the case.

Emma had been warned by her landlady to keep Stuart quiet as her husband couldn't get his sleep, so every time he started to scream with hunger she would dip a dummy in Lyles Golden Syrup and he would gobble away at it. The elderly doctor said that had probably saved his life, to get just a tiny bit of nutrition that way.

I was still trying to get leave with no luck, but because of my efforts the most shocking thing happened. In Leicester one night about 11 pm, two policemen came to the door. Emma nearly had a fit when she opened the door to see two coppers there, she thought it was bad news about me. They were there to check up on my claim for leave, but by then the critical point was over and Stuart was beginning to hold his own, so there was no hope of getting leave.

Homeward Bound

The rest of my time was in Poona on flying control. One shift in the control tower and one in a trailer type caravan situated at the beginning of the runway in use, its purpose was to be a last-second alert to the planes on final approach. When on night duty in the van as darkness fell, one duty was to start up a mobile 'Chance Light' and make sure the beam was working and shining down the runway. One evening I was doing this and two pairs of eyes, about waist-high, were shown up. I scooted back to the safety of the van looked out of the observation dome in the roof but could see nothing. They may have been small cattle, but I wasn't taking any chances as we had seen paw marks in the dust.

The other thing I remember was the arrival of Lord Louis Mountbatten, the head of all operations in the Far East. I was in the van at the beginning of the runway and was told on no account was his plane to be sent round again. He must be allowed to fly straight into land, all other aircraft would be cleared from the area. Just as I saw his Dakota appear, I spotted an Indian wedding party approaching to cross over just in front of the runway. I gave them a red warning light but they were all too tanked up and singing joyfully in their decorated bullock cart. They took no notice of the red warning light beamed at them even though there was a notice in Urdu telling them to wait if a red light was shown. In desperation I put a red cartridge in my Very pistol and fired, it landed just in front of the two bullocks, who reared up in fright and galloped off in the other direction. So the Royal Dakota came in and as soon as the wheels touched the ground a large Union Jack sprung up from the upper fuselage and all was well.

Eventually, my turn for 'repat' came up and we were despatched to Bombay for a final medical. After the medical, the guy said "OK that's done". I said "I haven't had a hearing test" as, over the years of flying in planes with no soundproofing I started with a ringing in my ears lasting for an hour or two, but in time it became constant. I wasn't after a pension but just curious to know what it was. We had never heard of tinnitus then. The guy said "You had the hearing test when you had your eyes tested" I replied that "You pointed to each line in the sight test". He replied "You can have a hearing test if you want, but if you do insist, you'll miss that bloody boat" which was moored in the harbour. I wasn't going to do that, but now if people are worried they are getting tinnitus I say

"You'll get used to it, I've had mine for over 75 years!" It is inconvenient though. I've always had problems at meetings or functions with a noisy background and tests have shown that I cannot hear the higher frequencies. The top five notes on a piano just sound like clicks to me. Thankfully, I can still appreciate music.

We caught the boat, but had we known, it would have been better to wait for the next boat, as the old tub we sailed on was an early coal-fired tall single-funnel passenger/cargo boat, the SS Lancashire. There was an old well known dirty song about a ship 'The Somersetshire', ours was of the same class. It was small, dirty and we were way down low towards the stern of the ship. We had a large tube running through at ceiling height, with the propeller shaft running inside it and in a storm in the Indian Ocean, when the propeller came out of the water the whole place shook like mad. She was also very slow and it took us three weeks to get to Liverpool during which someone had let seawater into the freshwater tank, which left us very thirsty! In Liverpool, we exchanged uniforms for a civilian demob suit and finally, I arrived in Leicester where Emma and our baby son were in an attic in a friend's house.

Every time Stuart whimpered Emma would go to

118

pieces, after what she had gone through it was not surprising. After a day or two we travelled up north to stay with my parents and they, as I had been, were shocked to see Stuart at seven months old, still looking like a little wizened old man. He must have looked awful five or six months earlier. However, he continued to thrive.

Emma had had an unhappy childhood, with parents at loggerheads and her father was quick-tempered and violent. Emma loved my parents and they loved her. On a previous visit to them, while I was still in India, they had gone for a walk one Sunday and saw a large house, apparently unoccupied, completely on its own in a little valley. I knew this house as it was only one mile from Foxholes, where my parents still had the little shop. This would be ideal as we had decided to try and settle as nearby as we could so that Mum and Dad would have Stuart to help after losing Alan.

At this point, I must explain that Mum and Dad, after receiving the first telegram about Alan, received a second telegram saying, 'Missing believed killed' nothing more. For the next few years after the war, I used to dream that he had returned, having survived and escaped into Poland, only to wake up and find it was just a dream which I found very upsetting. I had tried to find out more at the time but to no avail. Having previously been one of the first to the scene when one of our planes burst into flames as it approached to land it was quite horrible and for over 70 years I could not bear to watch any film or TV where there was a likelihood of this happening. Finally, after all this time an independent journalist who interviewed me over the phone was able to discover what had happened to Alan. He was a flight engineer in a Pathfinder squadron flying Lancasters, having done a tour of operations with Bomber Command flying Halifaxes. He had a 'rest' couple of months doing test flying and dropping 'Window' which was the code name for aluminium foil used to deceive enemy radar and was very effective. It was used to make it seem as though the landing forces on D-Day would mainly be much further north than Normandy. Thus the Nazi defending force was split and without it, the invasion forces would have faced much stronger opposition, with many more casualties.

On Alan's second trip with the Pathfinders, the Lancaster suffered a direct hit in mid-air and exploded. The only survivor was the pilot who was blown out of the cockpit by the force of the explosion and must have landed by parachute, but for the rest of the crew it would have been instantaneous and they would have known nothing. The journalist was able to tell me that Alan was laid to rest in the Marquise Cemetery in the Pas de Calais area and could tell me the row and the number on that row. Without this knowledge, I could not have written this book, so I shall be ever grateful for the peace of mind it has given me.

Alan Heath 1942[8]

---

[8] Alan's Lancaster ND736'G' took off at 22:58 on 19th May 1944 from RAF Oakington, Cambridgeshire along with 37 other Lancasters and 5 Mosquitoes to attack the Mont de Couple, Cap Gris-Nez jamming station. The jammer disrupted their bombing system causing them to miss the target by several miles. Alan's aircraft was the only loss that night. A second raid a few days later put the jamming station out of action for the duration of the war.

Back to Blighty

Back to late 1946 when we visited my parents after demob. Emma had previously sent me a letter to India saying she thought it would be an idea to try and get the keys to Ganton Dale House as it was called. I wondered how she would settle, a town girl, in a house with no mains electricity, gas or mains water, etc. It was completely on its own, our nearest neighbour was a good mile away. However, my dad had a word with its owner, a man living in a fine residence in lovely grounds, the owner of a large estate. He agreed to meet us and it was arranged for us to have an interview. He told us that he really wanted his gamekeeper to live there, but the gamekeeper's wife would not agree to live there with no facilities and only one country bus a week into Scarborough. So Mr Wrigley said we could live there for six months, rent-free so as not to create a tenancy, but with an agreement that we would move out, should he be able to get the gamekeeper's wife to live there. In return would we help by keeping an eye out for poachers, etc.

It was situated in a lovely winding valley, so it was a pleasure strolling round there. We were told by a local retired gamekeeper that Ganton Dale House had been a seventeenth-century coaching inn and was called the New Inn. There were two outbuildings still standing which were used by a neighbouring farmer to house some cattle but also some remains of more, which had perhaps been used as stabling. Also just in front of the house it seemed to sound kind of hollow and could have been a bricked-up cellar. At the time we often wondered what stories there might be, but it was probably as well, as years later we found out that it had a reputation for being haunted. Sometime after we left we heard that Mr Wrigley had sold it and the new owners had decided to open it up again as a roadside inn. I'm told that one dark foggy night a couple wanted a local taxi to take them, but the taxi driver said no, it was rumoured that a coach driven by white horses had been seen by someone! I do remember one evening when I returned from night classes in Scarborough, leaving Emma and Stuart alone in the house, Emma said she had heard a tapping on the downstairs window, when she peeped through a gap in the curtains there was a large white horse looking in. When I got home she told me to look outside with a torch. It had rained quite a lot that day, but I couldn't see any kind of hoof prints in the soft ground outside and next morning in daylight, not a sign and we heard no reports of a horse being missing. A final twist to this, the new owners opened up the access to the cellar and found a skeleton in there! A little way down the valley there was an oblong kind of earthworks, now grassed over, which was reported to be the remains of a cockfighting pit and one can imagine possibly the result of a wager going wrong maybe. I don't think it was ever solved, whatever happened.

At the time we moved into a section of the house, probably the servants' quarters, there was a huge old oven door, with a smaller door for the fire, with an even smaller door for the access to remove the ashes. When we moved in it needed a lot of cleaning and there was a greasy patch on one wall, maybe because leather harnesses had been hung there. We stayed for a total of seven years and only saw the owner twice: when the local hunt was passing and also when we handed back the huge key! But in that time we had installed Calor gas lighting and a cooker downstairs, and redecorated throughout. I also did the whole house externally as well. We were so grateful at being allowed to live there for so long.

One day when I was at work Emma noticed two rough-looking men outside the rear of the house starting to dismantle the hand-operated water pump. A tall affair with a long metal handle. She rushed out to stop them and they couldn't believe it was our only water supply. There was a very large dairy with a tall stone filter, but it took ages to get enough water and we didn't always have time to wait, until one Christmas when Emma's parents were visiting and they had brought a glass water jug and glasses as a Christmas present. We were just about to start Christmas dinner, using the new jug. It had convex curved sides which magnified the contents. Suddenly my father in law saw something moving in the water. We filtered the water through some muslin which left a pink film left there. After that, we used to bring drinking water from the village standpipe in a milk churn. I said at the time, those pink things were probably eating up the even smaller nasty things.

Having arrived back to Britain and making the move from Leicester to Yorkshire I then had to start looking for a job. The first firm I applied to was Slingsby Sailplanes at Kirby Moorside, about 30 miles from Ganton Dale. It had flying connections and I'd heard that they had just one test pilot and I thought that if they expanded I would be on hand if extra testing was needed. I went there to learn about the construction of their products and was elated to be accepted and started just after Christmas.

The only transport I had was a 1931 Zenith Jap 500cc motorbike, which had been Alan's before he sadly was lost in action. The bike had been kept in a damp barn for a couple of years and its magneto had suffered. In wet weather, it proved to be very unreliable, but we were so short of money I could not afford a new one. I would start at 6 am and if things went wrong it could be 11 pm or later before I got home. We could not find anywhere nearer to the workplace and as Stuart was still a baby, he used to be carried between Emma on the pillion seat and I, when visiting my parents or relatives nearby. On my travel to work I had noticed a sidecar frame, with no body, outside a small garage. I think it was £5 and so I bought it and bolted it onto the motorbike frame, but it had no proper sidecar lugs, so it was a bit of a problem. I had heard of a sidecar body for sale about 15 miles away and arranged to go and see it on the Sunday. I didn't want Emma to go as, with Emma on the pillion and little weight on the sidecar it could be a problem. However, Emma insisted so we started out. It sure was a problem when we had to do a left hand turn the sidecar wheel was up in the air and on one sharp left-hand bend, she had to get off and walk round. When we got there the sidecar body seemed to be reasonable so I bought it, also for £5 and made a temporary job of fixing the body to the frame. On the way home I insisted that Emma would sit in the sidecar which she did. All went fairly well until I heard a scream, looked down and the front fixing of the frame to the bike had given way. The sidecar was sending sparks up from the road and slowly parting company from the bike! I stopped and rebolted the front back, but this time Emma sat on the pillion! When we got home she said "You can take that damn thing off and sell it. I am NOT going in it again!" I did what she told me and put it out in front of the house and sold it for £12, so we were £2 up plus I hated riding the bike with the sidecar when you couldn't bank over for the bends.

It was after this episode that we managed to find a 1931 Austin Seven, a tiny saloon, for £80 which had been restored by a local garage owner. My parents helped by insisting they would go halves with the price and add another £20 to our tab which we had run up with them. Mum and Dad helped people when they were having problems but applied a limit to each customer. I guess we had exceeded ours! We used that car for seven years and it gave no trouble climbing up Staxton Hill every day and when it couldn't make it I knew it was time for a 'decarb' and valve grind. This was not easy at Ganton Dale with no mains electricity. Once when she failed to climb the hill I put it into reverse gear and went up backwards as reverse gear was lower than first.

Just after I got the Austin, at the end of January 1947 the snow started, it kept on and on and because the preceding weeks had been extreme frosts, the ground was frozen hard and the snow just laid around and increased enough to block the roads with drifts in our valley up to 25 feet deep. We were isolated for thirteen weeks and I had to fetch supplies on a sledge, mostly over the fields. This was the last straw and I reluctantly wrote to Slingsbys, giving my notice. Something I bitterly regretted afterwards. It had been so easy to get the first job, but it proved to be a different kettle of fish getting another in and around Scarborough in wintertime as it was such a seasonal town.

For weeks and weeks, I tried to get work. The only job I could have had was to repair cycles for £2-10s per week. Emma said you must not take it as you will be at a low starting point and labelled as such for the future. One day, after trudging through the snow for 3½ miles to get a bus, I left my wellies at the pub next to the bus stop, to travel into Scarborough to look for work.

Dad, Mum and Stuart in the snow at Ganton Dale House

I was walking across the Valley Bridge to a garage to try to get a job there. The pavements were slushy and I had holes in my one pair of shoes with cardboard inside, when a very well dressed lady, coming the other way said "Why are you not at work young man? You could be cleaning these slushy pavements". I dared not speak my mind and just walked on. Perhaps I should have, she might have had some influence and got me a job. I felt useless, unwanted and superfluous and at that moment I could have hopped over the bridge railings down to the road below, there seemed to be no hope. I felt that it

130

would have been better if I had gone and Alan, who would have had a brilliant future, had survived.

I had read that work was available in the Midlands and Emma and I felt that we had no option but to go down and try there, staying with Emma's parents. I had heard that Sir Stanley Black, the head of the Standard Motor Company was always ready to employ ex-RAF aircrew, so that was my main hope. When I tried to get an interview there was no way I could get near him. I also found that there were jobs available for maybe bus conductors, etc., but not anything with a future so, much to my parents' relief and of ours really, we returned to Ganton Dale and I carried on from there. Things were so bad I had to sell my drum kit and a second-hand trumpet I had bought in 1939 just to put food on the table and could not consider starting the band again. I needed a weekly wage and also half the band failed to return from the war.

Something Special

Eventually, I was lucky to get a job in a shop selling radios and photographic equipment. It was owned by a very nice gentleman who was nearing retirement age and his son was taking more responsibility. It wasn't really what I wanted to do, but I was so grateful. I was not a born high-pressure salesman and one day Mr Frank Slingsby's wife came into the shop and asked if I could help her buy a suitable camera for her husband's birthday[9]. I sold her a very good quality camera, which wasn't as complex as say a 35mm Leica, as she said her husband had no previous experience other than a simple folding one, so she didn't want anything too complicated. Afterwards, the boss's son wasn't happy, he said "You could have sold her a Leica, they could have afforded one". Eighteen months later Mr Slingsby came in and bought a Leica as he was now more familiar with the technique.

---

[9] Mr Frank Slinsgby was the owner of Slingsby Sailplanes who Brian had previously worked for.

The nicest customer I ever had was Mantovani, the band leader, who was playing a season at the Spa. Another very interesting man, but not so well known, was Cameron Earle who came to the shop to enquire if our recording system was portable to help him with his research work. He had a small section in a large garage in Scarborough doing experimental work. When I showed interest in what he was doing he invited me to go and see his place. He showed me a drawing in detail and asked me what I thought it was. I made a kind of inspired guess and said "Is it an infinitely variable gear unit?" He replied "You are nearly right, it is a variable gear but with a very wide range from high to low". He was chosen to write a brilliant book to cover the German all-conquering Mercedes and Auto Union development and he gave me a signed copy. He suggested if I were to do night classes in Engineering at Scarborough, he might be able to give me a job once he got the necessary capital to go ahead with his research. He went on a fundraising tour and tried to interest Bob Gerard, who had garages in the Midlands. He was testing Gerard's pre-war ERA (English Racing Automobiles Ltd) car at an airfield and it overturned and poor Cameron Earle was killed. A sad loss to the motor industry and especially the sporting element.

In those days it was black and white photography and when I heard that a gentleman who did all the enlarging in the upstairs darkroom was to retire, I volunteered to do the job. He taught me a lot and I found it interesting. Sometimes people would be using a camera with almost square negatives and they would want postcard size enlargements, it was very difficult to know what to leave out to get that shape and they might say "Oh you've missed out our favourite rose bush", etc. The other difficulty, people would take a photo of the newborn baby standing in a doorway in bright sunlight with a dark background, with the baby in a white shawl and it was difficult to bring up any features of baby's face, but there was also lots of really good ones.

At lunchtime, I would eat my packed lunch and read the Photographic Journal. I found that adverts for staff doing my job in other parts of the country were offering nearly twice as much money than I was getting and I asked the boss's son, who had now taken over, for a rise, but I made a big mistake. I said if I couldn't get a decent rise I would have to leave. He replied "OK, we will be sorry to lose you, but wish you well in your next position!" So I was out of work again. I learned a lesson, never give your employer an ultimatum.

Having worked all day in the darkroom I had lost a lot of colour and one or two people asked if I was ill. Our neighbouring farmer suggested he could do with an extra hand for the coming spring and summer so I started work on the farm. Hard graft, but I found it to be a healthy job and a good life if you wanted to spend your life outdoors. After the summer ended I was out of work again, but I then found a job as a fitter for a local firm of electrical engineers making all kinds of generating plant and I spent about five years with them.

Emma, Stuart and Me on Filey Beach

We were still using the tiny little Austin 7 hp saloon, probably the most reliable car we ever had, we travelled all over in it, but I had always wanted a sports car. We couldn't afford one so I decided to build one. We sold the baby Austin for £80 and I had to budget carefully to keep within this figure. We had moved from Ganton Dale in order to get Stuart a place in a decent school in Scarborough to get a better education. We lived in a council house in a village near Scarborough and I could walk to work from home. We had no garage to work in, but I was lucky, as one of my workmates lived with his family in a converted railway carriage, he had a small shed almost opposite from the firm where we worked. Also, next door to our works was a garage with a large scrapyard at the rear. For economic reasons and also that I knew the Ford 1172cc side-valve engine was tuneable, I decided to focus on that engine. The garage had a Ford 8 hp saloon which had been rolled and the body was beyond repair, but its owner wanted to keep the engine. I could have the rest for £5. One of the garage mechanics knew of an 1172cc engine with a cracked cylinder block, he also knew of a firm in Hull who could weld it safely and that cost me £10.

The next problem was where to build it. Again I was lucky, my workmate agreed to my offer that if I could use his shed I would in exchange put mains electricity from his house to the shed, with lights and 2 power points. So now we had premises. The only problem was the size of the shed, the width meant that you could only work on one side of the car, so it had to be pushed out and moved to the other side each time. The boss of the firm agreed to my working on the welding, if I paid for the lighting and gas used and if I bought the materials from the firm, i.e. metal tubing and sheets of aluminium, which I was happy to do. When I had finished the welding, with the help of a pal I'd made at work, the boss looked at it and said it would be too rigid and it would break up in six months, but my plan was to have a firm frame and make the road springs softer by removing the third leaf of each spring. I was lucky to have got the right springing and the 'Special', as we called it, was one of the best handling cars I've ever driven and it didn't break up!

I had read all the books I could on things like tuning and car handling, so it was a bit of theory, a bit of compromise due to the limited finances available and a bit of common sense. The other expensive thing was a twin-inlet manifold with two Aquaplane SU type carburettors. My choice of a Ford 1172cc engine was based mainly because the Aquaplane Company, based on the Norfolk Broads, were well known for tuning products as this engine was used for a cheap class of racing powerboats there.

They made alloy cylinder heads, manifolds and other bits to increase the power output. Emma and Stuart had saved up a bit of housekeeping and pocket money each week until they had the necessary £15 for the inlet manifold and carburettors, which were in effect SU Carburettors made under licence. I was really amazed and delighted when they arrived. I was able to, very carefully, open up the inlet ports on the cylinder block from 1" to 1¼" diameter and polished them to look like mirrors. I then made up a 4-branch exhaust system with a modified silencer, each with a perforated tube inside and 4 exhaust pipes out to exit just in front of the nearside rear wheel. This gave a length of individual pipe of the length I had calculated. This all worked very well and the power output that I got was better than I had expected.

All was going well, but up came an unexpected problem. I had read of an exciting project, the BRM[10] 16-cylinder racing car that was a potential world-beater. The brainchild of Raymond Mays who had sold his ERA concern to help finance and concentrate on the BRM. I wrote to BRM and said that I had no qualifications, due

---

[10] British Racing Motors was a British Formula One motor racing team.

to WW2, but was extremely enthusiastic and included samples of my drawings and photos of my two-thirds completed Special. I got a rather terse letter back, saying that they had got a team of highly qualified people who were also very enthusiastic thank you very much! I was disappointed but not really surprised, it was worth a try.

Wonderful Work

Three or four months after the BRM story I saw an advert in the Daily Telegraph, ERA were asking for qualified design engineers, offering a four-figure salary, which in 1956, was a good salary. With tongue-in-cheek, I sent them a similar letter with drawings and photos, etc. and much to my amazement received a reply suggesting my coming down to Dunstable where ERA were relocated after being bought by Leslie Johnson, one of the old school of gentleman racing drivers. I had seen him racing a Jaguar XK120 at Silverstone and ERA was now being used as a Research and Development project. I was well aware of the origin of ERA and its pre-war history, the first ERA was built in 1934 using a much modified Riley 6-cylinder engine in a chassis designed by Reid Railton. They built a total of 17 versions, mostly 1½-litre, but one or two with a 2-litre version. In the late 1930s to help continue financially, they formed an ERA supporters club, with a membership fee of 15/-. I joined and still have the little badge.

The letter I received was from their Chief Draughtsman. I couldn't believe my luck at even being considered. A date was fixed and I went down by train, to be met at Luton station, where I was approached by a charming young lady, who led me to a dilapidated looking Austin Cambridge saloon which looked as if it had seen better days. There was a winding country lane leading to the ERA premises on the A5 on the southern outskirts of Dunstable. When we got on to this road I just couldn't believe it. I was scared stiff as she raced down this lane, sliding the corners. I'd never experienced anything like it. What I didn't know was that the driver was the wife of John Draper, World Champion Motocross rider and the Austin Cambridge was an ERA modified job, with ERA designed De Dion rear suspension, ERA modified front suspension, an MGA twin-cam engine and gearbox. Talk about a wolf in sheep's clothing.

Then came the interview with Bob, the Chief Draughtsman and David Hodkin, the Engineering Director. I was delighted when it was over and they said they would give me a trial as a detail draughtsman, but if I wasn't up to it they could probably give me a job as a fitter on the shop floor. I would have swept the floor to be able to work in such a hallowed place! So it was arranged that I would start there in two weeks' time in order for me to give one week's notice where I was working. Although ERA told me that they were sorry that my initial salary would be low, due to lack of previous experience, they would revise it in six months if I was OK in the job, but even the starting salary was higher than I was getting 'up north'.

Now I faced another problem. If I was to leave the Special two-thirds completed up north it would never get finished, so I decided that if I could make it driveable I could then carry on finishing it in Dunstable and ERA gave me permission to house the car there and work on it in the evenings and weekends. This meant that all my good intentions to give it a good testing before putting it on the road had to be aborted and so its initial run on public roads was from Scarborough to Dunstable. I started out one frosty morning with no windscreen, just a little holder for the licence disc. No doors, they were nearly ready to fit, but had to be stowed in the boot which was quite capacious. I'd solved the problem of a fuel tank by using two Petter diesel tanks which were going for scrap, one behind each rear wheel, giving a clear boot space. We had to make it a three-seater, with Stuart sitting crosswise behind the two front seats, but we could also put a foam cushion in the offside footwell and seat two people facing the rear if necessary, or as a two-seater, we had a panel which would cover up the hole aft of the

142

front seats.

The journey to Dunstable went well but was rather cold! The only trouble I had was the condenser in the distributor failed and I had to keep stopping to clean the points until I could find a replacement, not easy on a Sunday. The first time the lads in the drawing office at ERA saw the Special they called it the 'cocoa tin car', it being unpainted aluminium. I managed to fit the doors and used a Vauxhall Victor rear window as a windscreen but hadn't got any wipers fitted when making my first journey back up north. There there were a few teething troubles but I had no time to fix them immediately. The main problem was driving in heavy rain, I found that with no wipers on the front screen the faster I went the clearer the top of the screen became, so it was a way of finding out the handling of the car in the wet! We had a soft top (removable hood) by this time but found the joints in the floor panels allowed spray to get in.

On one long trip, we found that the foam seat cushions, which sat on the floor to give a low seating position, were acting like sponges and after about three hours of it, I got out of the car to buy some fish and chips to eat en route. I didn't realise how soaked my trousers were and what a cold bum I had! I made it my next priority to seal up these floor joints, but in spite of this, we loved the car, which in appearance looked ahead of its time. Some people just pointed at it and laughed but others were openly in admiration. I remember one long trip up north in heavy rain and we were cold and wet, we stopped for petrol and a guy with a lovely Mercedes came across and was very complimentary, it really boosted our spirits.

The Special

The work at ERA was very intensive but really good. There was a wonderful spirit with very little discipline, there was no need as everyone was so involved and I had a very good section leader. It was a very small team originally and Ivor, my section leader, had only me as a section at first. It was the Chassis Section and we did everything apart from the engine and transmission section. The Body Section did the body and seating, etc. Ivor was very good to me, very helpful and he was always ready with advice and happy to explain things. I found that ERA had won a contract with BMC (British Motor Corporation), as it was then known, after a merger with the Austin and Morris companies, to design and build two prototype five-seater saloons, plus three more engine and gear units (the 378 Project). I was told that they would be a backup in case the Issigonis designed Mini and 1100cc cars, also brand new designs, were not successful. Of course it turned out that they were very much a complete success and our ERA design was completed but never needed. This was the reason that ERA needed more staff and I think that Bob took a big risk to give me a trial at the very early stage.

I had agreed to do two nights and one afternoon at Luton Technical College and made up for the afternoon by starting a half-hour earlier each morning. I was in digs in Dunstable to begin with and also doing some house hunting in the hope of buying our first home after 10 years. I had also joined the local car club where I met Peter Lockhart, an estate agent and a lady who was a solicitor with a Dunstable firm. Another member of the club was Peter's brother Frank, who had a garage in Dunstable and raced a vintage car. Peter told me there was a third brother who was an undertaker. Peter said "I find people a house, Frank sells them fast cars and Les buries them!"

When I told Peter that I was house hunting he told me a local builder was putting up a row of semi-detached houses in Kensworth, a nearby village and he could put my name down for the second house of the first pair. They were on a quiet road on the outskirts of the village, with open fields to the rear and a small group of trees opposite. Just what we were looking for. The cost would be £2,000 and we might be able to think about it if we could get a 90% mortgage as we had managed to scrape up enough. As it happened, a few years earlier when we were living at Ganton Dale, we had met a farmer, his wife and two young daughters on the beach at Filey one lovely Sunday afternoon and as we would be passing their farm on the way home, they asked if we would like to call and have a cup of tea and cake, which we did. We noticed about a dozen hens in a pen near their door and we were told that they were going to be put down as they were all disabled in some way. One or two had crossed bills and one only one leg and various other problems. We felt

146

sorry for them and asked if we could take them home. We did so and they thrived free-range with plenty of nice grass and they laid eggs really well, more than we needed, so we sold a lot and put money towards paying for my life insurance policy of £25 per annum. Up to then, it had been a worry to find the money.

When we tried to get a mortgage for the house in Kensworth I was told that, with my relatively low wage I could only get an 80% mortgage and only then if I could get a written statement from ERA that my salary was to be reviewed after six months and I'd only done about two and a half months at that time. I asked Bob if he could write a letter to that effect but Bob said "We can do better than that, we are happy with your work and we can offer you the raise right now!" What a lovely man.

Then another blow fell. I can't remember which party were in government then in 1956 but they announced that they were to introduce a credit squeeze, which would mean another £200 to find. Thanks to the insurance policy I was able to get an early sum from them and Mum and Dad insisted that a Post Office savings account which was in Alan's name was to be used. They were adamant that they would never use it and had finally cleared their loan from their bank and they were sure that

Alan would have wanted it that way and so we ended up with a nearly completed house. Peter had told me that the builder had underestimated the cost and sure enough, as the builder carried on down the road the price went up, so we had been very lucky.

Emma and Stuart had come down one week and we were in the front garden to be, when a couple from the village stopped to talk to us. When they found out I was in rather poor digs in Dunstable, Mary and Vic insisted that I went to stay with them. They had no offspring and I was more or less bulldozed into saying that I would. Mary was a very large lady and Vic was a well-built six-footer, his job was to fit rear axles to Bedford trucks, but Mary was the dominant one, what Mary said you did, no question. They were into old-time dancing and one night Mary said "You are coming with us". "Yes Mary" said I and during the evening she got me up on the dance floor. I was amazed that a person of such huge proportions seemed to just float along as light as a feather!

Mary worked at Whipsnade Zoo, in the cafe. It was only about 1½ miles away, she used to go there by bicycle. One morning she was stopped by armed keepers who said that a lion had been reported at large. Instead of cycling down a narrow path through the bracken, she was advised to keep to the main road, but Mary thought damn it, she would take the shortcut down the path. Suddenly a mane appeared above the bracken! She said her heart missed a beat, but then a head appeared, it was a Shetland pony, tawny coloured and quite docile. She got hold of it, mightily relieved and took it back to the keepers. "Here's your bloody lion", she said scornfully. I'd love to have seen their faces!

All went well with the house build and we were able to move in. The very next morning, starting at about 6 am, came truck after truck down the quiet country lane. We were totally unaware that further down the lane was an experimental department of Commer trucks doing endurance testing. It happened every morning but we soon got used to it and slept through it, but it was a lesson when buying property always do a good recce first.

One morning at work a guy came into the drawing office and said "Frank Lockhart's got an ERA for sale in his small showroom window for £40". My pal and I jumped into a car and went screaming down the road into Dunstable. On the way, we said we would throw in £20 each. Both of us were buying our first home and neither had a garage, but we would buy it first and worry about what to do afterwards. We raced to a halt, only to find that the price was not £40 but £400! That was a disaster as it was out of our price range. It was the ex-Arthur Dobson 2-litre and we could not possibly consider it. With hindsight, it would have paid us to sell our newly acquired houses and live in tents! You would probably have to pay a million for one today.

Another opportunity arose, one of the lads had bought a rolling chassis from ERA, the E-Type which was the last pre-war racing car they made and only two were built. It was complete except for engine and body. This lad had become very fond of a young lady, who had marriage in her sights, so the E-Type chassis had to go. He had only paid £100 for it and that was all he wanted. There was also a Riley 6-cylinder saloon for sale at the same price and this had the ERA modified roller main bearing. If I could get hold of an E-Type cylinder head it would be a great opportunity, but I just didn't have the money.

Nevertheless, it was sheer bliss working with such a great team of people, more than I could ever have wished for. One job I remember shortly after joining ERA was an example. We had a contract to test Avon tyres for performance and wear. We had a single-decker bus which had a wishbone suspension system grafted onto the nearside approximately halfway between its front and rear wheels. This was designed to be able to alter the castor and camber angles and slip angle whilst still on the move and all the forces were monitored electronically by Richard Hodkin, David's brother, who was a wizard on all things electronic. The designer of this gear was a great guy named Tom Cobley. I had been warned never to call him 'Uncle' as he was a black belt judo expert and could give you a hard glare with his tigerish eyes! He produced a felt pen sketch for modification to improve the system and my job was to make detail drawings of the components. As I was doing this I thought of a simpler way of possibly achieving the same object and with some trepidation, I showed it to Tom. He took a good look at it and said "I think you have got something there, we'll try it that way".

After 3½ wonderful years there we got some bad news. Leslie Johnson, the owner of ERA, had suffered a severe heart attack and his doctor advised him to sell up and retire to his house in the south of France. ERA was bought by a group of companies and we were led to believe that they had agreed to carry on with the ERA policy of design and development work as before. The 378 Project was completed on time and on budget. It was rumoured that David Hodkin had received a phone call from an American multimillionaire to design and build a world-beating sports/racing car, with money no object. This was turned down by the new board of directors and we believe that the American was Carol Shelby, who then got AC to do the job, hence the AC Cobra. We could have had that job but the new owner said no.

The firm also sacked the brilliant David Hodkin in a manner which, had it been a fictional story on TV, people would have said it was far-fetched. On returning from his final visit to BMC at Longbridge he was not allowed back into the ERA premises and his brother Richard had to remove all his belongings. They had trumped up a case against him, taking some of his remarks completely out of context and we were all dumbfounded. David tried to set up an independent small company to try and help his team, keeping them together, but wasn't able to get enough financial support. He had even suggested a new name for the project: Vehicle Dynamics, but as someone suggested, he was so focused on his work he hadn't thought about the initials the new project would have!

The new firm changed our initial name of English Racing Automobiles to Engineering Research Applications, but it turned out that all they wanted was the premises. ERA had been involved with the Rootes

Group in Coventry and had tuned and prepared three Sunbeam Rapiers for the Italian Mille Miglia and over the next few months David and Richard Hodkin, Jack Channer, our top chassis engineer and Ivor Bowness, my section leader, moved up to Coventry to work at Rootes. We were right in our assumption about the premises, in fact in less than two years the design office was closed down.

I started to look around and I had a word with Len Terry, who had been on loan to ERA from Tricorn Designs. He was very knowledgeable and was building his own designed sports/racing car in the living room at his home, having ensured that the French Doors were wide enough to get the finished car out! Needless to say, his wife left him during the build. The car was very successful and he built a small number of them, named after him, the Terrier. The racing driver and engineer Brian Hart won a championship in one of these Terriers. I told Len Terry I was considering applying to Lotus but as Len said they were paying peanuts, relying on people's enthusiasm and I knew Lotus started that way, so it put me off. I considered the local company Vauxhall which would have meant we did not need to move house, but was also put off applying being warned that there was a lot of internal politics. I found out later that the firm I did join was riddled with it. Len Terry later became Chief Draughtsman at Lotus and so designed the Indianapolis winning car along with Colin Chapman who was a genius! Len also designed the Eagle Formula 1 car for the American, Dan Gurney.

My greatest problem was that I was the wrong side of 30 years with no paper qualifications. One day I was lucky enough to get three job interviews in the same day. The first was at Aston Martin in the morning. I was offered a job in their Body Design Office, but body design is quite different to chassis design. Nevertheless, I was tempted when I saw two or three travel-stained experimental Astons in the courtyard. The salary was the same as I had been getting at ERA and I could have commuted without moving home. With hindsight, I wished I had gone there, but that's life.

My second interview was at the MIRA (Motor Industry Research Association), which started as a disused airfield and I had tried there once before when I made that unsuccessful trip from Ganton Dale to the Midlands. In those days it was not much more than the runways and a perimeter track but I wasn't offered a job then. MIRA had now been developed into a very technical place and I was surprised to be waved through the gate in the Special without checks. I found out later that the Special was so like the Sunbeam Alpine in appearance and I had no idea then that there was an Alpine in existence. As I was being shown around I was given the impression that I was going to get the job, so I left with fingers crossed.

The third interview was at Rootes where I was seen by the head of the Chassis Section. He asked me what sort of salary I was looking for. I gave him an annual figure, a bit more than I was getting. He replied "No we couldn't possibly give you more than £26 per week, which was more than the annual figure that I had asked for! I should have realised what a Fred Carno's outfit it was. However, the money was better and I didn't get the MIRA job, so I went to Rootes in Coventry, the sixth ERA man to go there, but nearly all of us were unhappy there. Most of them left, but I was stuck there and tried to tell myself that I was lucky to be there. I had not been able to continue my night school as Rootes wanted me to do three or four nights a week overtime and the powers that be had moved the goalposts for acceptance to qualify as an AMIMechE (Associate Member of the Institution of Mechanical Engineers). At my age, I was now not eligible.

My first job at Rootes was to do a large assembly drawing, using all the detail drawings to build an overall picture to discover any gaps or fouling of the different components and report them to the different departments. When finished I took a shortlist of body parts where there were a few problems on paper, as I thought that they should be put right before work was started to make the parts. Body pressings always give problems due to the flat sheet of metal being reshaped. It has memory, a tendency to spring back a little. This has to be allowed for when tooling up. The manager of the Body Section looked at my list, some discrepancies were quite small. He made the comment "You're like the bloody Japanese, on body parts we work to one–sixteenth". I could have remarked "Yes and then use tons of lead filler afterwards" but I kept my mouth shut. I could quote dozens of examples, but enough of that.

Life Number 8 - More Hot Stuff

I had only been at Rootes about eighteen months when I began to get health issues, headaches, stuffed up nose, etc. I was diagnosed with a Deviated Septum, which needed a small operation, about 2½ days in hospital. I was operated on by a 70 plus year-old gentleman along with two other guys with the same problem. After the operation, on the ward, the other lads were up after the first day or so, helping to serve tea, etc., but I was feeling worse. I got a rash all over and the doctor thought I was maybe allergic to penicillin and changed medication to streptomycin. Emma told a friend I was being put on strychnine and he said "That's a kill or cure job!"

My temperature started to rise. Two more doctors had a look, but no joy. Coventry hospital had been bombed and it was now located in wooden huts in a large park outside the city. Every time someone walked past my bed it shook and I was now feeling dreadful. My temperature was now 106°F and the last thing I remember was a very nice nurse packing my naked body with ice cubes and whispering nice things to me. I remember thinking I could quite enjoy this if I wasn't feeling so damn poorly. I then lost it and seemed to be quite detached from my body, kind of floating above it, looking down on this wretched soul in quite a detached sort of way. Apparently, they had called the elderly gentleman who'd done the operation at about 11 pm and he examined me, telling the other ward doctors "It's scarlet fever, see the strawberries and cream appearance down his throat". When I came round next morning the sister said "You have scarlet fever and you are being barrier nursed until you move to the Isolation Hospital". She also said "You haven't got it here, it must have been lying dormant until the operation gave it the right conditions". Apparently, they thought I wasn't going to last through the night. It would have been ironic if my first memory and my last were of an erotic nature!

Devastating Times

When I got back to work I was given a choice, a man from Marstons radiator manufacturers had convinced the Rootes management that they could build their own radiators with a new system of making them on a moving track i.e. more mass-produced instead of being virtually hand-built. They wanted a draughtsman to work for him in an office at Ryton on Dunsmore, where the big production lines were, to redesign the radiators on all the car range and also the range of Commer trucks. It wasn't what I would have chosen, but I wasn't happy where I was and Ryton was the next village to Stretton on Dunsmore where we lived, so it was much easier, no traffic queues and I got on well with my new boss. It was quite interesting to start from scratch, starting with an empty building. We got all the radiators redesigned and built on time and on budget, with all the machinery running beautifully. My boss told me he would soon be moving on and that I would be given his job. I doubt I would have got a new car every year as he had, but the pay would be very nice.

However, changes were about to happen, Chrysler

UK became the new owners of Rootes and they decided that the building we were using could earn more money as a paint shop and at a stroke, all our hard work was gone. I was back to square one and radiators and heaters were to be bought out again. For me, it was back to my old job and I'd lost two years of pay increases and seniority, it was a bitter blow.

An even greater blow happened a couple of years later. My dad was taken ill in mid-November 1964 and sadly died five weeks before Christmas. My mother went to stay with Uncle Ernest and Auntie Annie and we travelled from Coventry to Great Ayton near Scarborough for Christmas, only to find that my mother was poorly and when we got a doctor, he diagnosed advanced bowel cancer and in his opinion, she would be too weak to stand an operation, but it was left to me to make the decision. I spoke with Uncle Ernest and we agreed that we should let her stop quietly with lots of pain relief. Even so, I felt like a judge putting on a black cap – the worst moment of my life, but I was the only one left of our immediate family. One of her younger brothers thought that she should have been given the chance, but she passed away peacefully on the New Year's Eve. When the doctor examined her more thoroughly afterwards he said it was the best decision, she would never have survived such a big operation.

Emma, Stuart and I were devastated, both parents lost in just over a month. We never really recovered and I think that influenced a rather unusual plan of action a few months later. In the previous few years when money wasn't so tight, we had taken a holiday in Italy, always cheap ones and we had been to Jesolo, a cheap way of seeing Venice, which was easily reached by motorboats on the lagoon. We had become very friendly with a family who ran a smallish hotel in Jesolo. None of the family could speak much English and we, not much Italian, but the receptionist there was multilingual. They wanted to expand hoping to get more English guests. We did some research and eventually had three venues to look at, two in Italy and one in the Algarve. We planned to buy a left-hand drive VW Caravette and do a three months tour of Southern Europe, with the Jesolo one being the favourite. We sold our bungalow in Stretton on Dunsmore and nearly all our possessions. Stuart, our only son was working at the Atomic Energy Establishment at Harwell and was happily living in a hostel there and happy for us to do this thing. We didn't really have enough capital but wanted to give it a go.

We were staying with a friend in Rugby and were just

about to cross the channel when we got news that Emma's mother had also been diagnosed with terminal cancer and was only given three to six months to live. All our plans had to be cancelled. She did live a bit longer than six months, but by this time we were both too shattered to envisage our original idea and I was back looking for a job again.

My age and lack of qualifications meant no luck with three or four interviews, then out of the blue came a letter from Chrysler UK offering my old job back. I was glad to take it and we started house hunting in the Coventry, Rugby area. I was back in Coventry and Emma got a part-time job in Rugby and as we had loved living in the countryside up north and again on the edge of both Kensworth and Stretton villages, we were now living in a rented bungalow in Rugby. With money in the bank from the sale of our bungalow, we were able to buy a lovely Riley Imp two-seater.

While we were there I went down with flu. As I was recovering in bed I read in the local paper of a small farm coming up for auction. It was over one mile outside the lovely little village of Withybrook. I got up, dressed quickly and went to have a look. The farmhouse was not large and looked neglected but it stood back nicely from the road, with a small orchard in front. There was 56 acres of land, not a large farm and I thought it had great possibilities and when Emma came in from work, we went to have another look. There was a lot of work to be done, but we thought it would be something to take our minds off the previous months of sadness and disappointment at not being able to go to southern climes.

There was very little time before the auction and I applied to the HBS for a mortgage. They would give me a small mortgage on the house but not the land. My bank agreed to give us a loan on the land, but only if we could provide a signed agreement from a farmer to buy the land. There was another, larger farmhouse about 200 yards away and we found that originally it was one large farm run by two brothers. They had fallen out, hence the empty one which was for sale with a relatively small amount of land i.e. 56 acres. Mr Smith next door would have been very interested in buying but had recently bought more land from a nearby village so he could not consider it. The farm on the other side was just visible in the distance, the land came right up to the one we were interested in, so I tried there. John, the young farmer there, said they could be interested, but we would have to talk to his dad, who owned a large farm on the outskirts of Coventry and who had put up most of the money to buy John's farm. He said he would have been interested but had just spent a lot of money on a new milking parlour and it would be two years before he was in a position to spend any more.

I went to see our solicitor, who had handled our previous house transactions and we concocted a plan where Don, the father, could buy the land on a two year delayed completion and in order to create an agricultural tenancy, as an alternative he would pay the interest on the loan for two years. I'd got an estimate from Don as to what the likely sale price would be at auction, somewhere around £16,000 he thought. I drew up a sliding scale of what we would pay (a) for the house and two acres of land and (b) for the remaining 54 acres which would adjoin John's farm, the sale price running from £10,000 to £20,000. I put it to Don and he agreed but said if it reached more than £17,000 he would not be able to go any higher. If it went over £17,000 in total we would have to go it alone for the extra. We just had time for our solicitor to draw up an agreement but had not even time to get it typed out before Don and I took it to Lutterworth to see Don's solicitor to give it his OK. This was the morning of the auction in Rugby, so we raced down to Rugby, just in time for the auction to begin. En route we had decided that it would seem odd if Don didn't make a bid, so he would start and then drop out, leaving me to go ahead. When Don dropped out I came in with a biggish increase and the room went silent! I was dressed in a smart suit with a briefcase ready to go straight to work and as I was passing to do the signing I heard a farmer say "I'll bet he don't know one end of a chicken from the other!" Little did he know that I was born a country lad with both parents from a farming background. We got the farm for £12,500. I was a bit concerned that we had maybe not been fair to the seller, but he was the owner of a huge farm nearby and Don said not to worry, he's drinking himself to death and it would only be whisky money for him.

All went reasonably well during the two years, except Don and John had a bit of a fallout, so we were worried if it would affect things, but luckily they made it up and that was a relief. Then there was a change in the tax laws, which meant that we had to pay a bit more interest to the bank and there was nothing in the agreement to cover that. However, Don was brilliant and said that as we had agreed for him to pay the interest he would pay the increase. This meant that we had rather ambitious plans to greatly increase the size and modernise without losing any of its character. We went for broke and designed a

Georgian style house which would be appropriate for its location. We needed a large garage and workshop as we had acquired the vintage Riley Imp, I was also building a car to compete in vintage car racing. We needed a car each to go to work and I had bought three vintage motorbikes to be worked on as a retirement project. However, when we contacted two or three builders we could not possibly afford their estimates and their idea of a matching brick to the existing ones was not anywhere near enough for us to be happy with them.

In our rented bungalow in Rugby, the one next door was having an extension built and the bricklayer was a middle-aged guy who seemed to be doing a good job. We showed him a couple of the old bricks and he said "That's a Knapton brick", a small brickworks near Leamington. We took our sample brick there and sure enough, the foreman said "Yes they are ours and if you want some I will see them through the kiln, it's a bit like baking bread, the outside ones get more dark than the middle ones". He did a great job and we asked the bricklayer if he could take on the job for us. He said he would, his younger workmate, also a brickie would come, his nephew would do the labouring and he knew of a good joiner. We knew someone who could do the electrics and someone to do the plumbing, so we decided to do it ourselves at weekends and evenings where possible.

It took longer but we got what we wanted, it took 2½ years of hard work and not a few problems. When we had about three-quarters finished one weekend the middle-aged bricklayer didn't turn up. His younger mate said that he had got the opportunity to do a job which would mean he could set up on his own, but the younger guy said "It's OK we can finish the job". We thought it a good idea to spoil them a bit, warm soup in winter and ice cream in summer, but one hot Sunday I was toiling away hacking through an outside 12" brick wall and I thought I seem to be working harder than anyone. Then not long afterwards a friend phoned to say that they were having a drink in a local pub and they overheard these lads saying "We're on a good thing, we are going to make it last!" We realised they were talking about your house at Withybrook. The following weekend nobody turned up. I knew where the young brickie lived, so I locked up their tools in my van, went to his house and his wife said they were putting up a wall for someone. I dumped their tools there and told her to tell them not to bother coming to Withybrook anymore. John, our customer for the land, said "We can finish the job, we know a good bricklayer" and they did just that. So all was good in the end.

There was still a little to do, things like tiling in the bathroom, shower room and kitchen, but I had become quite good at that. We enjoyed another two years there. Emma was taking her Mini saloon into Rugby to work and I in my Minivan to Coventry. She told me about a Basset Hound, called Oscar, belonging to a doctor and his wife in Pailton, a village she passed through each day. Emma said that Oscar used to hitchhike to Rugby and he nodded his head to beg for a lift, she also told me he was sometimes to be seen in the bus queue in Pailton! I didn't really think he was so cute, but one weekend we were to drive to Banbury to celebrate our grandson's third birthday. There was Oscar, large as life hitchhiking. We picked him up and had the crazy idea of taking him to Banbury for the day. When we got to the outskirts of Rugby, Oscar got really restive on Emma's knee, he wanted out there, the reason, there was a butcher's shop opposite the bus stop! He settled down and so we arrived at Stuart and Carol's house on the outskirts. Pru and Fred, our grandchildren, were very excited to meet Oscar, who they had heard about from us. I was a bit worried that their garden fence was maybe not secure but everyone thought he could never squeeze through it. We were all sitting around when there was a wail from Fred in the kitchen. Oscar had found Fred's iced birthday cake and was demolishing it! Fred was crying, but we were all laughing and then Fred started to laugh too. Later in the day, Oscar went missing! Panic stations! Oscar had got through the fence and we started a search party, luckily we found him trotting away to the centre of Banbury! I was mightily relieved. I could visualise telling the doctor "I'm sorry we've lost your dog", "Where?", "In Banbury!"

Oscar was also well known to the staff in Rugby Hospital, he would turn up when meals were being served. There was also an incident in the village. A big wedding was taking place, with a marquee to hold the reception. Oscar had squeezed under the marquee and attacked the three-tier wedding cake! Opposite the butchers, in Rugby, lived a lady on her own. One night she was awakened by a tap-tap on the front door. She peeped through her bedroom window and there was Oscar, he'd missed the last bus out of Rugby to Pailton and after about 20 minutes she realised it wasn't going to stop so she opened the front door, in walked Oscar and settled himself on the hearthrug large as life! When Oscar died there was an obituary in the local paper.

Then came another blow, our life seemed to be like snakes and ladders.

A New Life

One night after visiting an old friend from her days in the WAAF, Emma was driving home on the A5 around 1 am, she inexplicably veered across the road just when there was a T junction on the right. As a result she ran into a brick wall head-on and this brick wall, about 3½ft high, edged a garden behind. The impact was so great that the windscreen shot out and was laid intact on the garden. Emma was not belted in and followed the windscreen out and maybe helped it out. The engine unit was pushed right back to the front seats and poor Emma had head injuries, a nasty wound from her left ear to within a quarter of an inch of her eye. Internal injuries, two broken legs, the left foot smashed up. The police contacted me in the early hours and said I should make haste to the hospital as she was in a critical condition. The last thing she could remember when she recovered consciousness next day was that she was driving on a clear moonlit night. Someone had phoned for an ambulance, but just left details of the place it happened and put the phone down, not giving their own name.

We will never know if she was avoiding something,

or just fell asleep, but afterwards for a long time if we were driving at night and a vehicle appeared over the brow of an incline she would panic and that was a similar situation to that when the accident happened. At first, the surgeon thought she would maybe lose her left leg, but after some months and more operations, they managed to save the leg, but her left leg was always a problem and in retrospect, it might have been better to have it removed.

After she left hospital on two crutches she was going to need looking after for a long period of time and so another decision had to be made. We had quite enjoyed the challenge of rebuilding the house at Withybrook and so once again I started to look for another run down or derelict property. We travelled along the Welland Valley as well as locally but could not find one at a price we could afford, allowing for the cost of restoration. Around that time an Aunt of mine who lived in North Yorkshire suggested that we might do better looking around there. She and Emma had been very good friends when we had lived up there. The outcome was that we took a look at things up north and we put our lovely house at Withybrook up for sale and I left Rootes to try our luck back in Yorkshire where property was much cheaper. I thought that there might be design work in connection with the newly discovered North Sea Oil, but in the event, most of the work went up to Aberdeen.

We found house hunting was much easier up north and, having found a buyer for our house, we bought our next house thinking we had a firm buyer for Withybrook. I bought a Commer van and car trailer to move ourselves from the Midlands to our new home on the northern edge of the North Yorkshire Moors National Park, roughly equal in distance from Whitby and Guisborough. It was surrounded by farmland with views of the moors one way and a distant view of the sea the other way. It took five journeys to complete the move due to the number of vehicles to be moved. We had just completed our final journey when we got a call from our solicitor in Rugby, that at the last minute the sale down there had fallen through. The buyer, who had given us such big talk and was immaculately dressed and told us he owned a mortgage company, had gone bankrupt! So we had to put 2 mattresses and cooking bits and pieces plus a Primus stove and go back to Withybrook and sell an empty house. They never look their best when empty. We eventually got a buyer from the Surrey area, where he was under manager for a big oil company and was just about to be promoted to become the new area manager in the Midlands.

I kept pestering our solicitor day after day until the contracts were signed and exchanged. The very next day the manager of the Surrey area collapsed and died. The company wanted our buyer to stay on as area manager in Surrey. When he told them he was committed to buying our house they told him to put it back on the market and they would cover any loss incurred. Our would-be buyer was also a vintage car owner with a big Alvis tourer and our four-car garage would be large enough to take it. With a shared interest we became quite friendly with them and some years later we invited them to have a holiday in a seaside cottage that we had restored, but not yet sold.

We still had enough capital left to buy another home and found one in Danby Dale, the house had not been occupied for some 40 years and needed a lot of work. Not only that but there was no road to it. The big thing in its favour was its location, halfway up the side of this lovely dale, with the most marvellous views. It was originally a handloom weaver's cottage, belonging to a family of Quakers. It included a small stone-walled uncultivated grassy area reputed to be a Quaker burial ground. If so, they gave us no trouble and it was nice to think that they were laid to rest with such glorious views.

We had to create a road over the moorland to begin with. We were lucky to find a young man with a digger who would take it on, but first, we had to get planning permission, plus approval from the North Yorkshire Moors National Park and lastly from a traditional group called the Court Leet. The latter proved very helpful and told us there was originally a track and we were shown boulders part worn by sledges, it was too craggy for wheeled carts. They advised us that the last bit up to the house was too steep and that the last few yards would be best done in well-ridged concrete, herringbone fashion, which proved to be a godsend. Once our road maker had got a rough road in place, he got a large mound of finer stone where the road branched off from the nearest metalled road, halfway up a steep climb. Every day we would fill a couple of bags of it in the open boot of our Mini to lay on the way and at the end of the day bring them back full of rubble from the rebuild to fill in an area that was very soft and boggy. It seemed to take tons of stuff before it became more stable and our road maker put in a large drain pipe which helped a lot. We had found a very good stonemason and his son, who was the seventh in line of stonemasons in the family.

We were demolishing a tumbledown barn which obscured the view up to the top of the dale and were using the weathered stone to build on a kitchen and an upstairs shower room and toilet. We noticed that Bob, the older stonemason was marking the outside surface of the weathered stone with a pattern called scutching. The newly marked grooves looked out of place on the old stone and Emma said to me "Go and tell him we don't like it" which I did. Bob replied "You may not like it now but if I were to come back in five years' time I wouldn't like it then" and carried on! Of course he was right and in two or three years' time, it had blended in with the rest of the house walls.

The water supply was directly from our own spring and it was a joy to drink, a missed opportunity there, we should have been bottling it. We had to get electricity from a supply nearby and there was no gas available so we had to use storage heaters. Bob recommended a tiler to sort out the leaky roof and add another roof over the extension. The tiler asked if he could bring his retired father to make a change for him. The old guy stood looking around and remarked "You are in God's pocket up here". The main problem was that it could prove to be inaccessible when really heavy snow fell in winter, so it would have to be a very special customer to want to buy it.

We had about £6,000 left after it was finished and about this time a cottage we admired was coming up for auction. It was right next door to the now disused lifeboat house on the quayside with external stone steps up to the living quarters. Foolishly I told Emma about it, having seen it in a local agent's window. I figured she would be mad if I had known and not told her about it. She was 100% in favour of living there, but I was a bit worried that it would break all the rules I had: one - not likely to be flooded and two - not subject to landslide. A lovely old lady was living at the other end of this row of cottages and she was full of stories about life in this smallish fishing village. There was a large unstable looking cliff at the rear of these cottages, with no access to the quay except through the properties and also a worry when storms brought huge waves in. Auntie Parkie, as she was known, said there was nothing to worry about and anxiously met us after the auction "Did you buy it?" she asked. Yes, we replied and she invited us in to celebrate with a cup of tea. As we sat there admiring her cast iron fireplace with a hood to help the smoke go up the chimney, there was a mark on this hood and she explained "that was when the piano was washed across the room and rubbed against the fireplace!" I said "I thought you said there was no worry about storms". She said "That was the big storm in 1953 and it will be only once in a lifetime". I said "Yes but it's my lifetime I'm worried about". She just grinned. We also found out that the ground floor of our new purchase was used to house a fisherman's small coble and it had burst out of the doors and been washed away never to be seen again!

We decided to carry on with the rebuild but I sure had reservations about moving in. As it happened, we ended up owning three properties, but with no money! So, we put them all on the market and it turned out the last one to be restored, i.e. Coble Cottage left us almost penniless after restoration. I saw an advert in Motor Sport, a Type 35 Bugatti for sale in Stokesley, not too far away. It was completely stripped down prior to rebuild. A wonderful opportunity to own a really classical model and priced about £1,000 less than Coble Cottage had cost us to buy. Nowadays it would be worth best part of or even more than £1 million, but once again, I hadn't got the cash.

It was always necessary to earn some money to help us in between house sales and I started to restore the vintage motorbikes and bought three more when one was sold, all needing restoration, also a Triumph TR2 sports car. I really enjoyed doing this work, but it is necessary to put an awful lot of hours into each project, so the rate per hour was low. I also did window frame repairs, secondary double glazing of my own design, waterproofing and flat roofs with GRP (Glass Reinforced Plastic).

A Sad Time

The worst job I undertook was to replace the broken metal lettering on a three-storey pub. Large ones at the front and smaller ones at the rear. A total of 22 letters in all and very few repeated ones, so they all had to be made by hand without a mould. The owner of the pub knew a guy who worked for a scaffolding firm and he would put up the scaffolding. When the letters were finished I arrived to fit them. There was a very long wooden ladder up to the front of the building and at the top a very narrow row of boards with no safety rail and when it was windy they tended to rock a bit. Then I found that the metal framework that the letters were fitted to was rusted very badly, but there was no way I could get welding equipment up there, so I had to clean it up and drill holes to bolt support struts where needed. I felt very unsafe up there and was very relieved when the job was done.

At one point, between selling one house and buying another we bought a second hand Lotus Europa. It was in need of a bit of work, but stuff that I could do and when it was sorted, it was the best handling car I'd ever driven. On a trip down the M1 to Oxford with our two grandchildren, one sat on Emma's knee and one between Emma and I. We were overtaken by an AC Cobra whose passenger was a lad, maybe a little older than Pru and Fred, our grandchildren. As he passed us our kids saw this lad making a rude sign and so they said "Go on, pass him again" which we did, but he then passed us again and I recognised him as being the owner of an AC Cobra dealership and of course the Cobra had an engine twice the size of ours and he was just playing with us. As I tried to pass him again I was aware that he had slowed down a bit and he was waving to me to slow, but too late I was committed to overtake him, only to find the car in front was an unmarked cop car, full of coppers and the three in the back seat were waving me to slow! They then indicated they were turning in to peel off at the next junction. I think I was very lucky to get away with it. But that trip down the M1 was the quickest I ever experienced, we were at our exit point to Oxford in no time. A light-hearted episode in a very busy life.

All the while I was caring for Emma, who was slowly getting better, until her toes started to curl up, due to a trapped nerve during an operation to remove a 16" long steel pin from her shin bone. This meant that her toe ends were very sore and bleeding. She arranged to have operations to straighten the toes with tiny pins in each one. I visited her in hospital and next day when I was on the way to Middlesbrough hospital to bring her home I got a flat tyre. I found that when I was changing the wheel I found it a bit more of an effort than usual, but thought nothing of it. Having got her home the following day I felt a bit groggy and thought I'd have a little lie down on the bed, but collapsed in the bathroom. Emma phoned the doctor and he diagnosed pneumonia. So there was Emma, trying to heel walk, not too difficult on one leg, but very difficult to do it on two. Somehow we survived but I found my right hand was very painful with the third finger a bit bent. I think I must have hit it on the toilet handle when I collapsed. The doctor said "You probably picked up the pneumonia at Middlesbrough Hospital".

But that was not the worst of it. When Emma was coming round after the anaesthetic, she kept saying "It hurts. It hurts". I thought she meant her toes but it wasn't. It turned out to be a pain in the bum! Its proper name was bursitis of the ischial tuberosity, the lower part of the pelvic bone which takes the weight when sitting. We were both having treatment at a nearby small cottage hospital. I was having therapy to heal my hand and Emma for treatment of her feet. Her treatment finished before mine and the sister said to Emma "Why don't you take a seat?" Emma told her she could not because it was too painful. The sister said she would take a look at it and that was the diagnosis. She asked "Have you had a fall on to your bottom?" "No I haven't" said Emma. "Have you sat for a long time on a hard surface?" Emma replied "No I haven't". She then said "I wonder if they dropped you in the operating theatre when you had your toes done?" That was when it started to hurt. We will never know but it affected her life completely, she never could sit for more than a minute or two and it never got any better.

We decided that perhaps we should start thinking about a move. By this time we had sold our second house. We were now in our early seventies and still living in our original purchase up north. Our son Stuart was living in Oxford and we thought it would be a good idea to move down to that area. We put our house on the market but it wasn't the best time to sell. The housing market had just about collapsed in the early 1990s and it took five long years to sell. We had three or four serious buyers but they could not sell their own property so it was stalemate. We kept lowering the price and then after four years, Emma had to have a big toenail removed. After it was done we arrived home just before snow started to fall! It snowed all through the night, with high winds and our access track, about a half-mile long, was covered in drifts waist-high. Next day and the day after we became more worried as the toenail removal had caused her toe and most of her foot to be inflamed and swollen. I phoned the surgery and they said to bring her in, so I explained that we were snowbound. They said if it gets worse and you can't bring her in we will have to send a helicopter. When I told Emma she said "A helicopter for a big toe. I'd never live it down". So I started to dig our way out, working from early morning to dusk. It took me three days hoping and praying that we didn't get a storm or high winds that could fill in all my work. Luckily it didn't and we managed to squeeze through and get to the surgery.

We decided that this must be the last winter there and dropped the house price still further. Even so, it was not until April before we eventually got a sale. Down in Oxford Stuart had found a storage unit for our belongings and he had a rented garage which he could clear so it would take the Riley Imp and two motorbikes, which were partially restored but needed finishing. We found a removal firm who were first class and everything went very well. The removal man told Stuart he had never seen anything packed so well, even colour coded so we could get at things most likely needed, whilst in store, as we had yet to buy our next home.

One big problem was that we had already found house prices in the Oxford area were quite out of our reach and it seemed that while in the north, as you moved further out from a town, house prices got cheaper, but in the Oxford area it was the opposite. As it happened I had noticed a hotel in Bournemouth advertising half-board holidays at what seemed to be a reasonable price and in the past where we lived you needed to keep an eye on the weather forecast and if there was a hint of snow it was wise to ensure you had fridge and freezer well filled and plenty of powdered milk, etc. But we'd noticed that, especially in winter, the best area in Britain for decent weather was in a radius of 15 miles from Bournemouth. We decided to take a long-awaited holiday in Bournemouth and whilst there, have a good look at the property situation.

It was late April when we arrived and it was lovely weather, small cafes with tables and chairs outside, with people sitting enjoying lunch dressed in short-sleeved shirts. We fell in love with it, streets lined with blossom trees, etc. and we started to go seriously house hunting.

Whilst the slump in the housing market had worked against us when selling, it had lasted long enough for it to enable us to get a foothold in the Bournemouth area, however we could not find a place that we liked and was in our budget for over three months and we were beginning to get worried as 'Sold' notices were appearing more and more often. In the end, we found a two-bedroom bungalow which needed a bit of work doing to it, but we liked the situation and it proved to be a good choice. The one thing we were not quite sure about was the very long rear garden, but I thought we could put it down to grass and I would get a powered lawnmower. Then our solicitor rang to say that he'd found a document which meant that we had even more land at the rear. After local enquiries and a good look at things, we were relieved to find that it was already incorporated. It meant that at one time there was a railway line between our bungalow and the rear fence. It was in a cutting and I'm told you could only see the tops of the carriages as they passed through. After Beeching, when the line was no longer used, the railway company filled in the cutting and offered the land to the property owners, which will give you an idea how long the garden was. It was a smallish two-bedroom bungalow with a normal size garage. Even though we were downsizing we still needed more space so we drew up plans to add a third bedroom at the rear, plus a small cloakroom, also to lengthen the garage to take our Morris Minor plus the

Riley Imp and two motorbikes. We found a young builder who gave us a very competitive price and he suggested he could put a pitched roof on the extension for a reasonable extra and this was within our budget if I drew up the plans, which I did. We got planning permission and went next door both sides to show the neighbours the plan and they were both OK with the idea.

Unfortunately, as we were leaving the neighbours Emma fell coming out of their door onto a hard driveway and suffered a pelvic fracture. She didn't have the best of luck poor lass and it was back to hospital, this time in Poole as we were living on the outskirts of Wimborne, a lovely town. Emma, who hated being ill, had not got the fighting power that she had after her big accident nearly 40 years earlier, which was still giving problems, mainly not being able to sit without pain. I can recall dozens of times when a nurse or doctor would say "Take a seat, Mrs Heath, we will be with you in a few minutes". She became more and more of a recluse and didn't want to see anyone, not even Stuart or her grandchildren, which made life difficult. However, we decided not to cancel the plans for the building extension and work began. We had become used to brick dust in our butter by this time! The third bedroom, a small hallway with a cloakroom with toilet and handbasin meant a rather narrow short passageway to a new back door leading to a carport in front of the existing garage. With some restoration of the bungalow and the new addition we reckoned we had doubled the value of the property and were very pleased with ourselves. But not for long.

Our life was again like a game of snakes and ladders. Emma developed a nasty left leg ulcer on the area of the leg where she'd had a big operation. We were having regular visits from district nurses and I took her to Wimborne Hospital once a month to see a consultant from Poole Hospital. The consultant eventually suggested Emma should go to Poole Hospital so she could see her more frequently. We agreed, but with hindsight, I wish I had said I would take her to Poole every day to outpatients because she hadn't been in Poole very long before she caught MRSA and then, even worse an obscure flesh-eating disease, which was very frightening. At one period when her wound was being dressed, the nurse got called away. I slipped in through the curtain to have a quick look. I am sure that I saw a small piece of shin bone exposed. Luckily they seemed to get rid of that thank goodness, but not the MRSA. I won't detail all the problems she had, suffice to say that she was a patient at seven different hospitals over eleven years, some many times.

I'll just describe two cases to show the type of hassle we encountered. One was after a long period in Poole Hospital, her strength and appetite was gone and if I wasn't there to feed her she'd not have eaten at all. The consultant was called and said that she must be fed by a tube up her nose and into her stomach. Emma asked what would happen if she didn't have it "You will die" said the consultant and she said to do it. I was there till late that night and she had had different nurses trying to find a vein in her arm to introduce a drip. They tried without success, eventually, I was told they had sent for someone who was the best in the whole hospital. This took about 1½ hours after which she was very upset. Then about 11 pm, I saw a nurse bringing a trolley with the equipment to put the feeding tube up her nose. I pleaded with her to leave it until next morning but she was adamant, she was to carry out orders. She tried and poor Emma was screaming "Help, Help, Brian help me". I felt awful, powerless because if I had tried to prevent it I'd have been banned from the hospital. Eventually, the nurse had to give up and I left.

The next morning I found that a different nurse had done the job without too many problems. She eventually gained some strength with the help of a nutritionist, the leg ulcer was getting so bad that, although she was back home it was decided that the only answer was a skin graft. She was referred to a specialist in Bournemouth and an appointment was made. She needed a stretcher ambulance and that was made clear when the appointment was made. On the morning of the appointment, the ambulance failed to arrive, allowing for the time of travel. I phoned the department and was told there was no ambulance booked for that day and I would have to make a new appointment. I said it was vital that she was seen immediately, she must be seen that day. After two or three phone calls they said that an ambulance was delivering a patient to Poole Hospital and then it would be directed to us. This meant we missed the original appointment time but the consultant made it possible to see her, although this meant he would miss his lunch break. When he saw her he said "Yes. You will need a skin graft urgently". Emma asked him how long it would be before she was admitted. He said "How about today?" it was that urgent. We agreed and she stayed there. I got a lift home, to return with her things.

After the skin graft her lower leg and foot looked so much better and the donor site, on the front of her thigh was about 3½" square. After a few days, she was moved to another smaller hospital to recover and because she had a history of MRSA she was in a room on her own.

Things were looking better, but the MRSA got into the donor site, also a pressure sore on the base of her spine. After some three months, she started to get small sores around the skin graft edge, but daily visits by the district nurses seemed to be keeping them under control. She was in such pain she was on Oramorph and then on a better morphine skin patch.

Around this time, after a long spell of dry weather, I was watering some plants by the front door and was taking the can round to the garage when two lads, who were about to knock on the neighbour's door, saw me. They said "Just the man we were looking for, we've lost our brand new football. We were playing on the bridleway and the ball went over the fence. Can we go and look for it if you open the gate for us?" I noticed one of the lads was hanging back, so I said "You both go back onto the bridleway and I'll look for your ball." We had once or twice had balls over the fence before, so it may have been possible. Off they went and I locked the back door and garage before going up the garden, as I suspected there was no ball to be found. One of them said "My mother will kill me, it was a birthday present, can I come in and look in your neighbour's garden?" "No", I replied "you will have to ask them". They wouldn't go, so I went to get a mobile phone and said "If you don't go

I'm going to phone the police" and I thought they had gone on along the bridleway. I spent a couple of minutes freeing a small lock on the gate, which hadn't been used for some time and then came back down the garden. Just as I was about to round the corner of the garage there was a loud crack and as I got there these two lads were racing off and leaped the front gate. I found that they had jemmied the back door and split it. Luckily the lock jammed into the wall plastering and the door was jammed tight, about two inches open but immovable. I was locked out and had no alternative but to knock on Emma's bedroom window. She was not quite bed-bound but found it a struggle to get to the front door and let me in. I phoned 999 and the police came, they were very good and I had to take the back door off its hinges to free it as it would not unlock from the inside. The door was split and beyond repair and the wall needed some re-plastering.

We don't know for sure if that was the cause, but Emma's back got extremely painful and it was back to Poole Hospital yet again. She came back home after treatment but was bed bound for the next eighteen months, when she got agonising internal pain, even in spite of the morphine patch. I phoned the doctor who came out and examined her. He called for an ambulance

191

and once more she went to Poole Hospital. It was an oedemic bowel and they operated on her that evening, but to no avail, she sadly passed away whilst being heavily sedated. I consoled myself by thinking at long last she is in no more pain. More than once, she had pleaded with me to give her an overdose but I didn't have the courage to do it.

A Road to Recovery

After a few months of being depressed, I thought I had reached a point where I was either going to go down and down, or I could do something about getting out of the doldrums. I had been troubled by arthritis, especially painful at the base of both thumbs. I needed two hands to carry a plate without risking dropping it. I dug out an old snare drum and tried to play it. At first, I could not hold the drumsticks, I had to bind the tops with Elastoplast. I practised for hours and found that it was helping the arthritis. Then I bought a cornet and practised that too.

I also went to the Allendale Community Centre in Wimborne and spoke to a guy in reception there. He suggested "Why don't you come to the afternoon tea dance to listen to the music, it's a live five-piece band and they are very good". I went and sure enough, the band was very good. I sat at a table on my own until the interval when two ladies, one youngish middle-aged, with her mother in law, who was 91 years old, asked me if I would like to go into the cafe with them for a coffee and cake as most people were doing. I went along and they introduced me to friends and everyone was very friendly with a really nice atmosphere. Because I had been playing in a band I never learnt to dance properly, so I phoned around to try and get lessons. At 86 years old the first two places I phoned were not interested but I did find one who turned out to be an excellent teacher.

From conversations with the band leader, there was a bit of a problem financially as there was the five-piece band to pay, also the hire of the venue and as I knew from past experience, publicity is all-important. I suggested to him that if he could get posters printed I would be happy to distribute them in Wimborne and the surrounding towns. It happened that the bass player in the band was a self-employed publisher and would print the posters. Michael and I became very good friends and when he realised that I was interested in jazz he introduced me to the U3A (University of the Third Age) and to Dick and his wife Isabel. Dick was the leader of the jazz appreciation class held every two weeks at his home and so numbers were rather limited, luckily there happened to be a vacancy. About ten of us were gathered there and as well as Dick playing some of his extensive collection, he encouraged us to bring something over. In that way, we got to hear a wider range of music. Small groups, big bands, early and fairly modern jazz. It made a very pleasant and interesting afternoon.

After one or two visits I gathered from the general conversation that one of the ladies, Margaret I found her name to be, went along every two weeks to the Durley Hall hotel in Bournemouth to hear live jazz by some of the best bands in the country. I didn't want to take my lovely old Morris Minor into town late at night. I knew two vintage car enthusiasts had had their cars vandalised at night in towns, anything a bit out of the ordinary seemed to be a target for the yobs. So I had to take a bus to Poole then change to a second bus to Bournemouth, but there was no late bus afterwards, so I asked Margaret if I could have a lift home. She agreed as it was not much out of her way. As it happened on the first night I missed the first bus to Poole, they had altered the timing but had not changed the board at the bus stop. I had to wait nearly half an hour for the next bus and by the time I got to the venue the band was playing the last number before the interval. I ordered a drink at the bar and I'd noticed the cornet player was playing a similar model to mine and when he came to the bar I asked him about it and how often did it need to be rinsed through, etc. He was very helpful and went to show me his cornet. It was a lovely old one but in perfect working order. He told me to always warm the mouthpiece before playing. He had a

Swedish wife and played a lot in Sweden. If they had an outdoor gig it was so cold he used a wooden mouthpiece.

I found Margaret during the break and we sat together and she dropped me off at my home afterwards. The next time I asked Margaret if there was anywhere I could leave my Morris Minor at or near her home if she would consider giving me a lift to the jazz in Bournemouth and back. She agreed and it became a regular fortnightly event. I offered to make a contribution towards the petrol but she said that she was going anyway and was glad of the company. We shared the same liking for different types of jazz. Margaret's husband had passed away about three and a half years earlier and I had lost Emma about seven months ago.

During the next few months, I was practising the drums and cornet and did one or two open mike nights in a pub in Wimborne. I wasn't very good but I got quite a lot of applause. A short time later I went to a care fair run by a local charity, Brendoncare. Lots of charities had stalls there. I asked about the various charities to see if I could do what I called a 'drumathon' and play for four hours non-stop. Of the various charities that I talked to the first one to contact me was the one I had hoped for, a children's hospice, Julia's House who do a wonderful job for children with tragic, limited lives and helpful support for their parents. They were having a stall at St Leonards Hospital who were having an open day to celebrate 60 years of the NHS and the opening of the hospital which was built by the Americans to house their injured personnel especially to be ready for the D-Day invasion.

Julia's House sent me a load of sponsorship forms and I went around the area with them saying I would be playing for £1 per minute. Emma had stayed at St Leonards after her skin graft and when visiting her I was curious to see large areas of old concrete flooring with shrubs growing through it. I was told that was the remains of a much larger hospital when first built, now much reduced in size. I suggested to Julia's House that it might be an idea to contact BBC South for publicity. They suggested it would be better if I contacted them. I did so and was very excited when they phoned back to say that Roger Finn, a cameraman and a sound engineer would come to my house on the Friday afternoon and I asked if it was shown, when would it be? They replied it would be the Friday evening. This was a good idea because the hospital open day was on Saturday, all day and quite a few people told me they had seen me on the TV and thought they would come along and support it. The hospital matron said I should be there by 8:30 am and start at 9:30 am. I didn't do my intended four hours non-stop, I did six! After four hours I was OK and as there were still a lot of people coming round I carried on. At a tea dance in Ferndown earlier I went around with my sponsorship forms and most people gave me something, but at one table of six people they said "We'll pay you when you've done it". I remembered that and at the next tea dance there I told them "I'd not just played four hours, I played six, so you owe me 50% more!" Most of them paid up and when totalled up it was over £500 for Julia's House.

The hospital matron had asked me to play as many American wartime tunes as I could and I had two Tommy Dorsey CDs with one or two numbers with a young Frank Sinatra on them. Luckily, when I was doing a musical quiz for a Brendoncare afternoon a lady came in with a small box of cassette tapes, early ones. She asked if anyone would like them, otherwise, she would bin them. No one else wanted them and so I took them. It was amazing, they were nearly all American Jazz of the wartime era. So at the drumathon, I was able to operate my CD player with my left hand, going from CD to tape, whilst keeping up the drumming with my right hand, so the music was non-stop.

On one of my musical quiz afternoons, because my quiz didn't take the whole afternoon, Brendoncare had invited a nurse who specialised in falls to give a talk mainly on cause and prevention. She asked everyone who had had a fall to raise their hands and then asked each one the circumstances and how it could be avoided. About a third of us raised our hands and she went from one to the next who mostly said it was due to loose rugs or bedlinen. When she got to me, she asked what happened. I said it was in my early twenties and I was absolutely stoned at the time – she pulled a face and said "I might have known!"

I had also joined the RAF Association and someone there suggested that if I was interested there was going to be a talk on the subject of radar development and progress during WW2. This was to be at Sturminster Marshall, a village near Wimborne and was a lecture by a Mr Bill Penley who was in charge of a section at the radar experimental group at Worth Matravers[11]. He was 91 years old and gave us a wonderful talk. He began by outlining the various attempts to give early warning of

---

[11] From May 1940 to May 1942 Worth Matravers was the nerve centre for radar development in the UK.

approaching enemy bombers, which had to be a worry before and after what was happening in the Spanish conflict. Various theories proved to be inadequate i.e. so-called 'death rays' and acoustics, but early experiments with RDF, as radar was initially known, did show some promise. With a small grant, I think it was £10,000 initially, it led to more success and hence the large pylon type transmitters were built and sited along the northeast and south coasts. I wondered if the German lads we had encountered at the Youth Hostel were connected with it. Mr Penley told us that before the war started the Germans sent an airship cruising up and down the North Sea to investigate why these tall pylons, as we called them, were built. Thankfully the scientists onboard decided that Britain must be expanding the mains electricity and got it so wrong. If they had made the correct diagnosis, at the outbreak of WW2 they could have bombed these radar stations when we didn't have the number of fighter aircraft to combat them and we would have lost the war. After the war, they showed the German scientists, who had been aboard the airship, their actual flight had been plotted and they were dumbfounded.

During the course of his lecture, he mentioned the Leigh Light Wellingtons and their effectiveness as a deterrent to keep the U-Boats submerged. I spoke to him after his lecture and he was very interested to know I had been using it and how effective it was. I didn't tell him, but we got a bit fed up with the fact that we kept having to get used to new modifications which came in often.

At a jazz weekend in Swanage, we were looking at the records of their work at Worth Matravers and I asked the curator if he knew how Mr Penley was doing. He said he was OK and suggested if we gave him our phone number he would pass it on to Bill Penley. After a week or two, we received a phone call from Bill to invite Margaret and I for morning coffee and it was a really pleasant morning. He described a good example of a typical reason why modifications were made to radar during the course of the war:

When we got radar small enough to be carried in planes and used to catch U-Boats, the U-Boat kills went up, but after a while, the plane would arrive only to find the U-Boat had made a crash dive and often just left a swirl. Our radar team concluded that the German scientists had devised a system where the pulse sent out by our radar was being detected and used as an early warning system. So our own radar wizards produced a new version to give a signal which became weaker the nearer we got to the U-Boat so that the Germans would think we were flying away from them. Our U-Boat kills went up again for a time until they got wise to it and so it was a continuous cat and mouse game.

Going back to 1944/1945, these modifications were so secret that none of us knew anything about them and we were fed up with the constant changes.

During this time I was taking dancing lessons and improving. When the U3A had an annual exhibition of their classes, during the break I sat with Margaret and her two friends. I hopefully asked if they were interested in ballroom dancing, the outcome was that Margaret and Mary came to an evening dance at Hamworthy Leisure Centre. As it happened there was an unusually long Wimbledon tennis final between Federer and Nadal, also an important football match, which needed extra time and penalties, so we got a very small number at the dance. This worked in our favour as Ron, a guy who had lost his wife about the same time as I had lost mine, and I were the only two men in the room. We danced with Margaret and Mary and as Margaret was quite tall and had a great sense of rhythm we danced pretty well together. I asked her if she would like to come and join me at my dance lessons. She agreed, much to my joy and my teacher, Pauline, thought it was a good idea. I warned Margaret that Pauline was a bit picky, "I like picky" Margaret replied and so we started going together. We soon began to improve our technique and try to learn new dances. We continued to go to jazz evenings in Bournemouth and Verwood and after a few months, I plucked up courage and asked if I could book for a jazz weekend, two single rooms, no hanky panky! This would be in return for her taking me to the jazz evenings, where otherwise I would have needed a taxi. After a little pause, she eventually agreed and I made the booking. By this time we had become very fond of each other and seemed to have so much in common. Margaret started to come to the afternoon tea dances, also to one in Ferndown and one in Bournemouth. We were dancing two or three times a week as well as the half-hour lesson each week. We were beginning to be quite good dancers.

The jazz weekend at the Roundhouse hotel in Bournemouth went very well. It was at this weekend I heard the brilliant Dave Shepherd playing clarinet for the first time. I had heard of him but had never heard him playing live before. I marvelled at his playing and also some of the other musicians. I told Dave afterwards that up till then I had believed that all the best jazzmen were born before 1920, but I have been proved wrong! We got to know him quite well over the next few years and he never forgot what I'd said. Dave was voted best clarinet player for five years running and he was known as the Benny Goodman of Britain. After one really good performance, I suggested they should be calling Benny Goodman, the Dave Shepherd of America". He said "You are too kind".

We decided to book another jazz weekend, sharing the expenses. We not only liked the same type of jazz but also the same with classical music. We went to a few concerts by the Bournemouth Symphony Orchestra. My dad ran the dance/jazz band, but his real love was classical especially the great violin concertos. My brother Alan was a lover of classical music and my mum liked the lighter side of classical and ballet music.

Margaret and I were spending more and more time together and after I told her about the wonderful scenic railway line from Fort William to Mallaig, we planned to take a holiday which contained the best, most scenic rail routes by rail one way and return by road. We really enjoyed it and I decided that if this Scottish holiday went well I might suggest us getting together, but at 87 years old it would be asking a lot and I put off asking her until after another jazz weekend. When I plucked up courage and asked her if she would consider marriage, or if not, sharing the same roof. She said "Give me a week and I'll give you my answer". I knew she was going to see her son for a few days and for me, that was the longest week of my life. When we met she said she didn't want the fuss of getting wed, but that she would be happy for us to share our life together. I was over the moon and as I had a huge garden it was best for me to sell and move in with Margaret. It was the best thing I had ever done and we have had eleven years of loving harmony. As well as the perfect emotional side which is wonderful, the fact that we now share expenses means that we have been able to take more great holidays.

Through the jazz holidays, we have made some great friends, both musicians and fellow enthusiasts. We share CDs, books, etc with two special friends, John and Brenda, who we met at Swanage Jazz Festival. John's father was a Japanese POW fighting in the Far East when his ship was sunk. His friend, who was retreating further and further to the stern of the ship as the water came flooding in and the ship was tilting more and more nose down, ended up in the engine room, thinking he was doomed, when a ships stoker shouted "follow me" and he knew of a ladder which went up inside one of the funnels and so he escaped. He was captured and because he was a tall lad the Japs beat him up a lot to show that although they were smaller, they were the masters.

Happiness

After about eighteen months of enjoying the afternoon tea dances at the Allendale in Wimborne, Michael, the band leader, told us that there was the possibility of getting a grant to help with the financial problems that they had. He asked me if I would be interested in forming a committee which was necessary to apply for the grant. I asked Margaret if she would be secretary, she already was secretary of Wimborne U3A and she agreed. I became treasurer and one of the other dancers became chairman. Because of my early experience in the 1930s, I was well aware of the value of publicity and when I bought a cornet and started to teach myself at the age of 87 I told people that my aim was to play it on TV when I was 90. I didn't quite make it, I was 90 plus 3 days before I appeared on BBC South. To get more publicity I had contacted them and told them that there were three people who were 90. A lovely lady used to come with her daughter and son in law and I found that she was born on the same day as me in 1922. She, Marjorie, used to sing with a band and loved the music and go around the room on her Zimmer frame in the jive! Also, the tenor sax player was 90 and started playing in a band in the 1940s. The BBC sent Ben Moore out with a sound and cameraman and they spent nearly all afternoon there. There is a lovely shot of Marjorie's daughter dancing the Veleta with Ben, saying "We turn now". I played 'Margie' on the cornet for Margaret and Marjorie and her son-in-law sang her favourite song. It was a lovely afternoon as well as being great publicity. We were lucky to be accepted for the grant and Margaret and I ran things for the next eight years.

The Dorset Community Foundation were very helpful each year with a top-up grant to make good our losses as attendance figures gradually dropped a little due to people of our age group having health problems. One day I got a phone call from the Dorset Community to say that in a 'Seeing is believing' exercise seven or eight of their committee or trustees would like to attend our monthly tea dance in July. Of course I said we would be delighted to welcome them, but privately I was very worried as July is usually our worst month for attendance figures due to holidays and people looking after their grandchildren whilst their parents are on holiday. Our worst ever attendance figure was nine and I didn't want to see almost as many members of the Community Foundation as there were dancers!

Due to my previous experience, albeit in the late 1930s, I knew that publicity is vital, so we went to town and emailed everyone on our list to support us if possible. I also got a small piece in the local newspaper that I would greet them with a musical tribute on my cornet. There was a problem though because Margaret and I were staying at the Queens Hotel in Bournemouth for a jazz concert all week and the tea dance was on the Wednesday afternoon. Because, especially at my age, I need to keep my lips in good shape, I took my cornet to the Queens Hotel and had a short blow on it on the Sunday, Monday and Tuesday. I kept it to within 6:15 to 6:30 pm so as not to disturb people in adjacent rooms, as the evening meal started at 6:30 pm. The great trumpeter, Kenny Ball, once said "If I miss practice for one day I know about it, if I miss two days the rest of the band know about it, if I miss three days the audience will know about it."

On the Wednesday, we drove from Bournemouth to Wimborne and I planned to have a run through with the band before the dance started as I'd never played with a live band before. However, when Margaret and I arrived half an hour before the dance was due to start we found that the people from the Community were already there, so I had no chance for a warm-up with the band. I had chosen two tunes with appropriate titles. Fortunately, we had a good attendance of dancers, nearly 50 plus two or three non-dancers who liked to listen to the band. When it was due to start I had a brief word "A warm welcome to our visitors and on behalf of all the dancers I would like to play 'When Somebody Thinks You're Wonderful' and the second one, if it wasn't for your generous support we would all be sitting at home singing 'Don't Get Around Much Anymore'".

It wasn't my best performance because I started to listen to the band, instead of blowing away and letting the band follow me, but it went reasonably well and afterwards, one of the lady trustees said "You can't be 94, you must be 84!" I was tempted to say "If I am 84 that means I was flying Wellington bombers when I was 10 years old." However, the whole afternoon was a big success and they left saying they were inspired, which was very good to hear. They asked me if I would attend their annual meeting to give a short talk outlining what we were doing, which I was happy to do. They also put my name forward to be included in the Independent newspaper's list of 50 happy people! This came to the attention of the Independent journalist who phoned to ask me if he could give me a short interview over the phone, he sent a photographer who took a photo of me playing the drums. This resulted in a half-page feature in the Daily Express.

The next opportunity to get more publicity occurred when we were delighted to get a small group of residents and their carers from a care home in Ferndown. We always charged half price for care home residents, carers were free, and love to see the happy smiles as they listened to the band and recognised tunes they remembered they had heard in their heyday. Margaret and I were surprised to see two of the residents dancing with their carers and even more astounded when we were told that Peggy, one of them, was 105 years old! She didn't go all round the room, but just along in front of the bandstand. At the interval, I thought that as I was 95, if I were to dance with Peggy we would together have 200 years 'on the clock'. Before the second half, I asked Peggy's carer if I could take Peggy on the dance floor. She said "As long as you are very careful with her as she is very precious to us". I promised I would be and asked the band if they could play the tune 'You make me feel so young'. The pianist rolled off a couple of bars, saying to the rest of the band "Foxtrot, B flat" and off they went, never having played it together before, but they were fine. I took Peggy onto the dance floor and expected to just hold hands and step in time to the music, but Peggy

211

wanted to come into a proper dance hold. She knew the steps and kept perfect time. I felt her trying to raise my left arm, I did so and she did a twirl to the right and then to the left. We were not going all round the room but moved quite well. The look of absolute joy on her face is something I'll always remember and it made all the effort of running the dances, with Margaret's help, worthwhile.

When the band were about to start the last waltz, we saw the party getting ready to leave so Margaret and I went over to say goodbye and ask if they had enjoyed it. Margaret asked Peggy if she had enjoyed her dance and Peggy, having heard the word dance said "Shall we?" so Margaret said "Go on then, have the last waltz with him" so we had another one where we doing gentle forward and reverse turns, she must have been a brilliant dancer in her younger days.

The more Margaret and I are together the more we enjoy each other's company and long may it continue, but as I am now 98 we live a somewhat quieter life. For the last eight years we have been taking a holiday in late February in the Canary Isles to enjoy some winter sunshine, but this last February I did not feel like the hassle of the airport and the four hours flying so regretfully decided not to go this year of 2020. As it happened we could have been stranded due to the Covid-19 outbreak and now we are housebound. I think the one thing we have found is that there is a great spirit by the British people. We have at least four people who have offered to do shopping for essentials for us, something we are tremendously appreciative of. Due to our relative inactivity, I have been able to devote more time to this writing and we have been able to look back at the wonderful holidays we have enjoyed over the last twelve years. I was so fortunate to have met my lovely Margaret.

Over the last 74 years, since I left the RAF in late 1946, I have been so involved in so many different ways to survive due to lack of qualifications and make a better life, that I had lost touch with my relations. About two months ago I was passed an email asking if anyone could put me in touch with Andrew Sefton, who proved to be my first cousin once removed, the son of Dot and Walt who I loved and it was Dot and her sister Freda who saved my Life Number 2. Amazingly at the same time my son Stuart sent us an email from John Kane, cousin Freda's son, asking if he was one of the family and I have now been in touch with both Andrew and John. They have sent me some rare photos which I had never seen before and I have been able to send them some which they had not seen. Unfortunately, my hearing is not so good and I have a problem answering the phone even though we have one which amplifies the sound. I look forward to making more contact with them but I haven't any computer skills and I am still a member of a dwindling group 'Men without Mobiles', though I will admit that they can be very useful at times. I am looking forward to seeing if any of the family have compiled a family tree, although with my mum being the eldest of a family of twelve and Dad the eldest of nine it's going to look like a family forest! In the meantime, I hope to emulate one of the well-known jazz pianists who, when asked to say a few words at his 100th birthday party, said "If I'd known I was going to live this long I'd have taken better care of myself !"

Wheeling and Dealing

I thought it would be fun to add a list of things that can happen to a 'nutcase' like me in pursuit of wheeled enthusiasm. The first happened just after the war, when I called at a country garage near Market Weighton East Yorkshire, to get petrol. I saw a lovely, but a bit battered Alfa Romeo Zagato bodied two-seater. On enquiring about it I was told that it had been owned by an American pilot who had rolled it, with some damage, but repairable. Sadly he was killed in action and they were holding it until its legal ownership was established. In any case, I had no money.

Years later in Dunstable, I was enquiring about a Riley Imp two-seater which was advertised locally, I was shown a collection of cars by the same owner, but they were all rotting away in his large orchard. He was just buying them up as investments, with no intention of using them. One was a dilapidated Alpha Romeo saloon which he claimed had the same chassis as the Zagato bodied two-seater. I told a colleague at work who was a great enthusiast and like me believed that vintage cars should be used and cared for. He asked "Have you got his phone number?" which I had. He phoned the guy and said "I know of a Zagato body in quite good nick, it's at an obscure (fictitious) address on the West Coast of Ireland". The guy jumped at the bait asking "What's his phone number?" My pal said "He's not on the phone, it's a very rural spot". Whether he actually went on a fruitless mission we will never know but it would serve him right if he did.

The next episode was more successful. As mentioned earlier we were only able to buy when we had sold a property and had not yet bought another. This time I was looking through the 'for sale section' of the latest Motor Sport monthly magazine when I saw a Riley Imp for sale. It was Sunday morning and we had just started to cook the Sunday joint. I phoned the number and the result was, we turned off the cooker and jumped into our Mini en route from Rugby to a village near Shrewsbury, about 85 miles away. When we arrived it was a lovely old house with an interesting history, it had taken refugees from London escaping the Black Death. A very nice couple and their son, who had decided to sell the Riley Imp. It was in a not too bad condition, certainly within my capacity to restore. The main problem was that the young man had fitted the wrong size of wheels and tyres. The rear ones were too small but with big fat Michelin X tyres. The front wheels were the right size but the tyres were over large. However, we loved the look of the body and agreed to buy it. We left a cheque as a deposit and arranged to collect it the following weekend and pay the balance. We did that and as we were about to leave I was impressed by the mother's concern, she said I do hope you have a good journey and do give us a ring when you get back home. I said I would and we had a good trip home. When I phoned her she seemed so relieved and I wondered why, we had done about 85 miles with no problems, with one stop about halfway to check that Emma was following in the Mini. But afterwards, we found the reason for her concern. After we had done about 45-50 miles the engine would falter and then stop. After checking, when everything seemed OK, she would do another 45-50 miles and then stop again. Two expert Riley guys could not find the solution. I had already tested the electric fuel pump to fill a large bottle without a problem. In desperation, I tried it again, this time with a five-gallon can. After it had pumped about a gallon of petrol the pump slowed down and stopped. The fuel pipe came to the top of the tank at the rear of the car. I got a length of plastic fuel pipe and connected it up. This time no problems so I knew it was the copper fuel pipe. At the top of the tank the pipe had a fairly sharp bend where the round shape was slightly flattened in section and some misguided person had fitted a tiny piece of filter gauze where the pipe was connected to the tank and it had been sucked up to this point where the pipe section was slightly flattened and was stuck there. After about 45-50 miles of running the bits of fluff and debris in the tank built up behind the gauze and blocked the flow of petrol and as soon as you switched off the ignition the built-up residue dropped back into the tank and allowed the petrol to flow again. Once this was sorted we had another problem, someone had opened up the jets in the two Zenith carburettors, probably trying to solve problem number one and so the mixture was far too rich. One of my Riley experts offered to sell me a pair of SU carbs, an optional extra when the car was sold new and I liked the SU carbs better so I fitted them. My other pal, a true Riley enthusiast, found a pair of front tyres and I'd found the correct rear tyres and wheels, which transformed the handling from good to superb. We enjoyed the car for over 40 years.

An amusing episode in the 'good old days' when the MOT meant a road test (before the rolling road now used). I was driving with a tester in the passenger seat with a device on the floor to record the braking, on a long straight with no other traffic in sight he said "When I say stop please brake as hard as you can." When he shouted stop I hit the brakes and he shot forwards and hit his head on the windscreen! No problem there he said. The front brakes had been made better by lengthening the operating lever and at one VSCC (Vintage Sports-Car Club) meeting, where vintage cars were in a small car park behind the main stand, two guys were looking at the lever and asked if this was the car that had raced a Snetterton some years earlier. I couldn't say as I didn't know its full history.

Me at the wheel of the Riley Imp

The road going Riley Imp was a bit too heavy for its engine size but Riley made a version, the Ulster Imp, which was more competitive. Due to Emma's health problems we hadn't used the Imp on the roads for the last 12 years or so, but when we sold it I was happy that it was going to a good home and would be used properly again.

By this time I thought I'd like to get a car suitable to race in vintage events and began once again looking through the adverts in Motor Sport and other magazines. I found one in Motor Sport, a special bodied Lea Francis rebuilt by Beatrice Schilling. I knew of her, she holds the lap record for the Brooklands circuit on her 500cc Manx Norton. I was still working at Rootes and living in Rugby at the time. I phoned the number in Bournemouth and said I would come down that Saturday and pay the advertised price which was not too high. They agreed and I said I would arrive in Bournemouth about 1 pm. If anything cropped up to delay me I would phone them and they said that was OK. When I arrived there I was greeted at the door by a guy who said we have a bit of a problem, there were two people, father and son, who claimed they had been before, agreed on the price and bought it, they had returned with a Bankers Draft to collect the car. However, another person had been earlier that morning, who had agreed to pay £100 more and had left a cheque with them! I had a word with the husband, whose wife was selling the car and asked if it was the car owned by Beatrice Schilling who held the Brooklands motorcycle lap record? He said "Oh fancy you knowing all about Auntie Beatrice! I do wish that you could have the car!" The couple were not really greedy but had no business sense whatever. I offered them another £100 on top of their best price and left my phone number and said "Get in touch if you can sort the legal position out." Needless to say, I heard no more, a wasted journey.

I later found out that Beatrice Schilling worked at Boscombe Down Research centre during WW2 and one of her brilliant ideas was to solve a problem with the Spitfire and Hurricane fighters in the Battle of Britain. They both had Rolls Royce Merlin engines which had their petrol feed through carburettors. Their problem was that in high G manoeuvres the G force meant that petrol was draining from the carburettors back towards the fuel tanks causing a loss of power when it was most needed. The German ME 109 fighters had direct fuel injection and did not have this problem, giving them an advantage. Beatrice solved the problem with a brilliant idea, so simple, often the best. She put a small washer in the fuel pipeline, with a large enough aperture to give sufficient petrol for maximum power, but small enough to restrict the amount of petrol draining back in high G situations. This was, somewhat rudely, named Beatrice's orifice! I think it was Sydney Camm, the Hawker designer who said "Simplify and add lightness".

My next case was a Scott motorbike advertised in Motor Cycle News by a guy living in Bradford. I was living in North Yorkshire, near Whitby and agreed to go over and see the bike. It was pretty well in bits with one or two items restored, but most needing work to be done. We agreed on a price and I told him that I would hire a van and collect it in two day's time. I left a cash deposit and suggested that as the petrol tank had been nicely restored I thought it would be a good idea to take the tank with me in the Mini with it wrapped up in an old blanket that was in the car. This meant that it would not get scratched in transit in the van. The deposit would more than cover the cost of the tank. He said he would rather not. I should have insisted but I didn't. I rented a van on the day and collected it on the morning. I was shattered when the post arrived just before I left home. There was a letter from this guy and enclosed was a cheque for the amount I'd paid as a deposit. He had decided to carry on with the restoration himself! I was furious and as I had an appointment with my solicitor, regarding a house transaction, I asked him for his opinion as I was sure we had a legally binding contract. He agreed but advised against it as the legal costs might be higher than the bike was worth. He then suggested I should send the guy a bill to cover the cost of van hire plus my wasted time and petrol and we agreed that £60 would be a reasonable figure. I did this and got a second letter and cheque with a note accusing me of moral blackmail!

At one stage we had run up an overdraft with the bank and I told the manager that we would clear it when I sold the Triumph TR2 car that I'd spent hours restoring. We had previously sold four motorbikes at auction by one of the big auction houses and these specialist auctions were held in the Midlands, while we were still living near Whitby. I thought we had a great relationship with the auction house and if I could not go down for the auction he would know the sort of price I aimed for, but without a fixed reserve, so that if the best bid was say, up to £20 off my expectation to let it go as it would cost more to go down to collect the car. It had worked previously and this time I had a bad back and couldn't attend. I'd expected to get about £2,500 for it and when I rang him up after the auction asking him if it had been sold he said yes it had. I asked him how much and was astounded when he said £500. I gasped, but he said "There was no reserve, what could I do?" They get your confidence and then bang! Nowadays they have a better system, with a reserve, but 10% discretion. I was furious and as I had an appointment with my bank manager very worried about not being able to clear the overdraft. He was none too pleased when I told him what had happened and I was forced to sell two unrestored motorbikes to get some cash in. In the next Motor Sport magazine, a South coast dealer showed a photo of the car, price £2,500!

I have mentioned about the type 35 Bugatti and not being able to buy it, so the next one was when I had to sell the Lotus Europa, which I was only able to buy as it needed a lot of mechanical work that I was able to do. When sorted it was the best handling car I'd ever driven and was said to be the nearest thing on public roads to the Formula 1 cars of the day, except for the top speed of course. I had to sell it as the insurance kept escalating. I advertised it in Motor Sport and got a phone call from a guy in Barnsley. He had a fairly high pitched sort of voice and I imagined a smallish mild-mannered type. We were travelling down from Whitby to Oxford to visit Stuart and the family and arranged to call and see this guy on the way home. We were not in the Lotus, but in our Mini. On the outskirts of Barnsley we stopped to ask a small group of kids who were playing nearby for directions. They said second left on then on the right-hand side, but one of the little girls said with a grin "You want to watch out cos he's got a lion! and it got out a couple of weeks ago." I remembered reading about it in the Yorkshire Post and he was only allowed to keep it if he beefed up the cage, which was quite large, more like a small yard. When we got there it was true and there was also a very ferocious Alsatian dog on a long chain, with only about 18 inches to squeeze through to get to the house. When he came to the door he turned out to be a big strapping guy, completely the opposite to what I had imagined. He said the Lotus was not for him, but for his son - "I call 'em flying coffins". Anyway, we could not do a deal as he wanted to include a Hillman Avenger plus cash, but in no way did we want another car. There was a huge scrap yard behind the house and before we left he showed us a lovely old Rolls Royce 20 saloon in the corner of a large shed full of bits and pieces. Afterwards, I said to Emma "It's as well we didn't do a deal, if it had gone wrong we might have seen a van coming down our farm track with his lion inside!"

The next possible customer for the Lotus was a youngish lad from Leeds. As it was quite a distance to travel we arranged to meet up halfway in the car park at Mount Grace Priory which was open to the public at weekends. The Lotus was only insured for me to drive, but I gave him a run around a roughly 30 mile circuit of winding country roads and because I thought it may be the last time I drove it I really pushed it along. The young man was very impressed and we arranged to meet there in a week's time when he would bring the cash, with a pal to drive their car back to Leeds. I drove the Lotus with Emma driving our Mini. When we met up in the car park the whole area was deserted and his pal turned out to be a wise guy type. He tried to get the price down although we had agreed on the price the week before. He even tried to criticise the handling, which showed him to be just trying it on. Then after about 20 minutes of haggling, he suddenly reached down, removed the keys of the Lotus and went over to say something behind his hand to his pal. I realised we were in a vulnerable position, they could jump into the two cars and speed off without us receiving a penny. That's when I opened the Mini's boot and removed my shotgun! I said "If you value your kneecaps mate, you'd better put the Lotus keys back and the pair of you get out of my sight while you can". Before we left home, I had a last-minute thought and put the shotgun in the Mini and boy was I glad I had done so. On that rather dramatic note, I will leave you.

But not before one last amusing story. We replaced the Lotus with an early split-screen Morris Minor. We bought it from a young couple who had neglected it very badly, but we only paid a low price for it, probably the number plate was worth the price I paid. When we bought it, on a rainy day and it was parked on the road, so I couldn't do a lot of checking. However, I crawled underneath and rapped on the chassis with a large screwdriver. It seemed OK, but when it went for an MOT it failed and we found that someone had put a strip of metal plate onto the rotten bit of the chassis but had stuck it into place with polyester resin! The garage said it was not worth repairing, a write-off. I took it home and remembered that in a monthly newsletter from the North East Morris Minor Club if you need welding ring Trevor. I did so and this young man came out and said "It's bad but I've done worse and I could do it for £250." I said that I wouldn't want to pay for it and it still not go through the MOT. He said OK pay me when you have got the MOT which I thought was very fair. I took it to the small lock-up garage where he worked and he did a great job. We ended up running her for over 30 years and we got to really like her. Quite a different way of motoring to the Lotus, but it gave us a lot of pleasure.

When I moved in with Margaret who has a 1993 Vauxhall Cavalier, another lovely car we still run and enjoy, Margaret said we could put the Minor in the garage and keep the Cavalier in the drive, but I said no and decided to put the Minor up for sale. I was in a charity shop one day talking to one of the staff who liked Morris Minors and said that as well as the car there was a lot of spare parts in the loft that I had accumulated over the years and I would need help in getting them down. A young man overheard our chat and said he would be interested in buying it. I told him the asking price of £1750, he looked a bit surprised so I explained "One, seven, five, zero". He said OK and came to look at her that evening, he had a little test drive and said "Yes, I'd like to buy it. Can I start to help you get the stuff out of the loft?" I asked him "How do you intend to pay for it?" and he said cash – he then produced a £20 note and held his hand out for some change! I stood aghast when he said "You did say £17-50 didn't you?" I couldn't believe it, but sent him packing!

Image Credits